Thoughts I've Had

Volume I

By Shannon Nixon

Chapters

Part I

Thoughts I've Had That Show I Think Too Much | 5
Thoughts I've Had That Reveal How Little Time and Energy I Devote to Personal Hygiene and That I'm an All-Around Abhorrently Disgusting Human Being | 16
Thoughts That Expose I'm Secretly a Crotchety Old Man in a Female 20-Something's Body | 22
Thoughts That Prove I'm Still Trying to Get it Together | 32
Thoughts I've Had When I'm Being Socially Awkward | 45
Thoughts I've Had That Prove I'm Delusional | 54
Thoughts I've Had as an Insomniac | 58
Thoughts I've Had Since First Moving to New York | 60
Thoughts I've Had on the Subway | 64

Lazy Thoughts | 66
Thoughts Regarding my Relationship With Food | 71
Thoughts I've Had in Yoga Class | 76
Thoughts I've Had at The Dentist's | 79
Thoughts I've Had on a Blind Date (Round 1) | 82
Thoughts I've Hand on a Blind Date (Round 2) | 85
Thoughts I've Had on a Blind Date (Round 3) | 87

Part II

The Time I Broke My Leg in a Rock-Climbing Accident in Spain and was taken in by a Former French Foreign Legionnaire Named Jean Claude | 90

The Doctor, The Pitbull, And The Girl Who Snuck Into a Fashion Show | 112

Impromptu Hitchhiking | 116

The Flavio/Fabio Italian Love Triangle | 123

The Cop And The Crack Whore | 131

Taco Michael | 141

The Handsome Pilots | 146

The One Story I'll Never Fully Understand Myself | 150

The Time I Thought My Friend Was Being Raped And Pillaged by a

Stranger So I Obviously Called 911 | 157

Stacy, You Stupid Woman, You Owe Me $200 | 162

The One Time in My Life I Felt Like I Was in an Episode of Friends | 165

Running Over Traffic Cones at 1 AM is as Fun as it Sounds (Possibly

Illegal as Well) | 169

Turkish Delight | 175

Thoughts I've Had That Show I Think Too Much

I never understood the concept of elaborate, foo foo weddings. Why drop $30,000 for one day? How tasteless. My wedding will be tame. I'm not even going to wear a wedding dress. Just black leather pants. And my bridesmaids will also be wearing black leather pants. And after the priest marries us, my bridesmaids are going to walk the groomsmen back down the aisle on leashes. And when we all get to the reception, I'm gonna have a Big Mac buffet. Can you imagine? Walking into a beautiful reception hall and there it is in all its glory: hundreds of Big Macs piled on top of each other.

Pooping is natural, but pooping on a bed is unnatural...I should be writing Chinese fortune cookies.

I wish a cop would pull me over so I could strap on my handcuffs and just sit here with a look of bewilderment upon my face when he comes to ask for license and registration. Maybe I'd get a date that way.

I am never going to understand how men can do splits.

I wonder if I'll blow up if I fart on that heater.

(Staring with a furrowed brow and unabashed disdain at women's chests as I pass them in the grocery store) Bras are prisons for breasts.

Someone just left a bulldozer unattended on the side of the road. Are they asking me to play with it?

Miss Nixon will never find a suitable beau with that ghastly set of eyebrows she has. Poor pet. While the men go out in the field and the factories to work, she is at home, burdened with the monotonous chore of manicuring herself. Every day, she must address those beastly things upon her face lest she die a spinster. Although, Miriam, at her advanced age of 23, I dare say she already is one…why am I narrating the simple task of plucking my eyebrows like some gossipy, cucumber sandwich-eating, Elizabethan parlor society bag?

Today I feel like singing Italian arias. Now, which ones do I know? Oh that's right, none of them.

If anyone wanted to torture me for information all they would need to do is lock me in a room with them and chew with their mouth open. The sound of lips smacking together is a slow death. Start doing that and I'll tell you anything you want to know.

Why on earth would anyone buy mittens when they could just stuff their hands down their pants?

There is nothing more disrespectful than some snot-faced little twerp rolling their eyes. And not just at me. When I see them do it to anybody. I instantly hate a person who does that, whether there is a legitimate reason to roll their eyes or not. You look like an annoying, condescending brat. Anytime I see a person roll their eyes I wanna bop them on the head and watch their eyes roll out of it. Now this *(points to my own face as I do a disapproving side glance)*, this is not an eye roll. This is a look of disdain. I do this all the time. *(I'm in the shower during this entire rant. I suddenly realize that I am having a full-fledged conversation by myself)* Who are you talking to? What do other people do in the shower? They probably clean themselves.

Wait…what? Drake and Josh aren't friends in real life? Total douche move of Josh not to invite Drake to his wedding.

…this is what you choose to think about during the day? This is exactly the reason why you haven't become anyone important yet. Change your thoughts and change your life.
(Five minutes later)
…But if I *was* a teletubbie, I would be the red one.

People who complain about how hard it is to have children are bizarre. Isn't the whole point of having children free slave labor? Why bother having them if you're just going to let them turn into entitled little brats who you coddle and do everything for? I get that you have to take care of them when they are babies. Obviously, you can't just let them die. You'll go to prison. But once they are old enough to walk, aren't they old enough to start walking your plate from the dinner table to the kitchen sink? Seriously what is the point of kids if you don't have them do all of the things you don't want to do?

Once upon a time there lived a young fairy princess in a magical kingdom with skin as white as snow, hair as brown as mahogany, and nipples as pointy as lawn gnome hats. Every morning, she would wake up and tweak her nipples with BIOFREEZE in order to maintain long-lasting nipples that could melt steel beams. She did this with the hope that one day prince charming would come riding in on his white steed searching for the fairest maiden in the land with the perkiest nipples…yeah, I really should be thinking more seriously about writing children's books.

My eyebrows are the primary reason why I will never reproduce. I look like Cara Delevigne's homeless sister. No. Worse. I am the lovechild of Groucho Marx and Brook Shields if Groucho Marx and Brooke Shields were cousins. My eyebrows make up at least half my face. They are caterpillars on steroids.

They've made like 17 "Pirates of The Caribbean" movies. I remember watching the first one as a kid and fantasizing about one day having a part in the franchise as a spunky lady pirate. Fifteen years later and they're still making them and I'm old enough to actually be a spunky lady pirate in the movies. Just like Keira Knightley. Man, I remember how big they made her knockers look when they put her in that corset. I can't believe she was only 17 in the first movie. Don't think about a 17 year old girls boobies, Shannon. That's rapey. Except in the state of New York, I guess. See, I could get away with a revealing top. Because I'm a grown up and my breasts are legal. Plus I wouldn't even need a corset with my naturally busty double Ds. Ok…maybe my double B's. Or A's. Whatever. I don't know. Why do you always bring it back to boobs?

Come rain or shine, inside or outside, I will always wear big, black sunglasses. I used to think I did this to be fashionable like Anna Wintour. I now realize I do it to cover up the bush twins on my face.

(Drops trousers and plops on the can, sighing exasperatedly) I'm 5'6. I look like I'm 5'4, which irritates me because I'm 5'6. I measured myself like 15 times today and I'm definitely 5'6. I'M 5'6! *(Looks around)* You are now at the point where you speak out loud and have conversations with invisible people that you think are in front of you. Also, 15 times? People are going to think you don't have a job.

They all told me that by a certain point in my life I'd change my mind about having biological kids. I'm 23 years old and I still have zero desire to bust a watermelon sized human out of the most delicate orifice known to mankind. Which is actually incredibly reasonable, in my opinion…but just to be sure, I'm gonna watch a home birthing video.

(Watching home birthing videos) Why am I watching this? OH NO PLEASE, GOD, NO THERE IT IS. There's the kid. Everyone's crying because they are so happy. I'm crying because I'll never be able to un-see that again.
…I love the internet.

(In my room, alone, eating rice pudding, I abruptly look at my closed door) You know when you really think about it, it's weird that people just take metal sticks and put them inside the hole in their face and then pull the stick back out, put food on it, and shove the stick right back into their hole. Over and over and OVER again. And we pretend this is normal? Wait a minute…I'm talking to a door again…

(Staring out my bedroom window, waiting for my Amazon Prime package to arrive) That little boy is just adorable. I love his little outfit. Those

grey pants are so stately. They make him look like a proper English gentleman. And that hat! He looks like Christopher Robin with that rain hat on...which is weird because it's sunny out so he shouldn't be wearing a rain hat. It's also a bit odd that he's just standing there so peacefully by the side of the road. Kids never stand still. Where are his parents? He hasn't moved in like five minutes. *(Puts on my glasses)* Wait a minute. That's a fire hydrant.

Of all the things my ex did to hurt me, mispronouncing the word sandwiches was the worst. I can't even begin to explain how much I wanted to curl up and die every time he said "sammiches". Buddy, did you not go to school?! There are literally two times you should ever be saying "sammiches": IF YOU'RE FIVE OR IF YOU'RE FIVE. I still lie awake in bed some nights steaming about it. It's been three years. I just want to sucker punch you in your sammich-eating face. GO TO THE LIBERRY AND LEARN HOW TO READ!!!!

Thoughts I've Had That Reveal How Little Time and Energy I Devote to Personal Hygiene and That I'm an All-Around Abhorrently Disgusting Human Being

Febreeze is basically the same as perfume and therefore spraying Febreeze on myself before going on a date is perfectly acceptable. And if I get my pits with this wet wipe I don't even have to shower till Tuesday.

From this day forward, I am a new woman. And as a brand new woman I am going to start taking pride in my appearance and personal hygiene. I'm actually going to wash, brush, blow dry, and straighten my hair all in the same day. Then I'm gonna spritz myself with a lovely free sample of some crap I swiped from the Macy's makeup counter and apply a light, effervescent dusting of tastefully done, very natural-looking makeup.

My Dad's reaction to seeing me after cleaning myself up: "Shannon! What is on your eyelashes?! You got some weird black stuff on them that's making them curl up. What is that?!"
Me: I'm wearing mascara…

(In line at the store) Ugh, what is that awful smell? Somebody in here WREAKS. Can you seriously not CLEAN YOURSELF?

How hard is it? People DISGUST me. *(the moment of realization)* Shannon, put your pits down.

Look Shannon, you got this girly haircut so you could style it and do things normal girls do with hair. It's been two weeks and nothing. You haven't even brushed it. Can't you at least run a comb through it?

My morning beauty routine consists of wiping the mascara I slept in off my face with my finger and putting deodorant on when I remember.

Remember last night when you were in the shower and you thought it wasn't necessary to shave your armpits? Good job, now you have to walk around with your arms by your side all day long.

(Has a Jeff Daniels from Dumb and Dumber moment. On a train. A Moving one. After the explosive diarrhea, I open the thin door that separates the train bathroom from the passenger seats. There is one man sitting directly across from the bathroom and he is a stud. He is looking directly into my eyes with a face that contains both horror and sheer disappointment. I smirk at him.)
You betcha, buddy.

That is either a baby tooth or a booger in my beverage. Either way, I'm still drinking it.

Front wedgie, FRONT WEDGIE! So. Uncomfortable. Just yank it out. This is Wal-Mart. You're fine.

(On the pot, reading statistical facts about pooping habits) People spend 5,749 hours of their lifetime pooping. Double that for me.

Every time I eat takeout, I find a human hair in my food and every time I keep eating it.

I was right. Enya and pooping…you really can't have one without the other.

(Sniffs armpit) Good. I remembered.

Shannon, don't force it because it might not be a fart.

Little girl running to her mother filled with euphoric glee: Mommy! Moooooooommy! I farted and I pooped my pants!
Holy crap, this child is me.

(Sneezes violently at Red Lobster) Ok, I just pooped myself a little bit.

(Eating soup that I ordered from a takeout restaurant. Midway through, I find an EYELASH. Stares at it intensely for nearly 30 seconds.) This is a pinnacle moment. I can either throw this soup in the garbage where it belongs or I can continue eating it. Well, I've already been eating and who's to say there isn't a bevy of other eyelashes in here? I'll just keep eating it.

Thoughts That Expose I'm Secretly a Crotchety Old Man in a Female 20-Something's Body

(Walking through Anthropologie) Oh, how I loathe this place. How gross. I bet this was made by a child slave in Myanmar and the corporate stooges of Anthropologie marked it up 3000%. If I could get away with doing anything I wanted to and had limitless amounts of money, I would take this $99 dish towel that's really worth $6 and wipe it between my butt cheeks after eating sixteen Frito Lay burritos from Taco Bell right here in front of everyone.

Inspirational Meme: You did not wake up today to be mediocre.

Me: Yes I did.

Me: Nobody loves me. I'm gonna die alone.
A boy: I'll go out with you.
Me: No, not you.

(Driving behind somebody who should not be driving) That was beautiful. Why don't you just completely stop in the middle of the road before turning left next time?

(Getting fed up with girls who hate me because I have boobs) One more time, I'll say this one more time:

I "free-ball" my boobies solely for your benefit. That is correct. God created my breasts for the sole purpose of stealing your boyfriends away from you and I acknowledge this by doing my duty of not wearing a bra. I shoot laser beams out of my nipples that hypnotize your boyfriends and make them leave you for me. You could say I'm a boobie super villain and my super power is my nipples.

Naturally, my choice to not wear a bra has nothing to do with me. It's all about you. Because it's always about you. The whooooooole wide world revolves around you and your huge, fragile ego. Now go cling to your boyfriends real tight, cuz the girls and I are gonna be out in full-force in a few hours.

(An odd-mannered, eccentric gentleman takes it upon himself to kiss the fair lady's hand at the time of meeting her) RAPE MY HAND WHY DON'T YOU?! Buddy, I didn't even let my own mother kiss me goodnight as a child. What makes you think you can just saunter over here and go in for the kill, you unapologetic turd-flavored pervert?!

Why do people think that just because they are walking diagonally across the road as slowly as humanly possible with their pants hangin' around their under carriage looking like a thug that I won't hit them? Listen, bro, you don't know my life. I will hit you with this minivan.

(On the porcelain throne in a public restroom, reaching for toilet paper and coming in contact with a strange, cold, slimy, and crusty substance...this is a true story) What the---NO! NO NO NO NO! Some classless barbarian went digging for gold and yanked out a sizeable B-O-O-G-E-R out of their filthy, low-life nose, wiped it on this once fresh piece of toilet paper, and LEFT IT THERE. I JUST TOUCHED SOMEBODY'S BOOGER. I TOUCHED A BOOGER!!! I TOUCHED A BOOGERRRRRR! THIS IS MY LIFE. THIS IS MY LIIIIIIIIIFE!

Stranger asking one of the most cliché questions of all time: But you are so pretty! How could you be single?

Me: Trust me when I tell you that I'm ugly on the inside.

Guy I have never before seen in my life: You look unhappy. Smile.

Me: This is exactly what my face looks like…

Somebody younger than me called me "honey" three months ago and I'm still stewing about that. I need to text my therapist.

(The lid on my McDonald's salad is not securely fastened and three dollars worth of salad paraphernalia falls out everywhere) THIS IS EXACTLY WHY YOU DO NOT GET PAID $15 AN HOUR.

(Roommate's cat begins screaming at me incessantly) Shut up, cat!! Stop whining! I will EAT YOU! God made animals so humans could EAT THEM. Not just cows and chickens…CATS. Don't believe me? You're not just a house cat! YOU ARE THE BACKUP FOOD, KITTY! When Armageddon happens, WE EAT YOU!!!

Is it rude to offer strangers deodorant? Surely it would not be as offensive as their odor.

(Belligerently drunk fellow hits on me relentlessly at the local watering hole) If you don't stop speaking, I will literally bite my own arm off just so I have something to throw at you.

(An oaf of a woman takes up the entire shopping aisle with her cart, oblivious to the fact that other humans exist and need to get by her. I forcefully ram my cart into hers)

Me: I'm sorry.

My brain: No, we're not.

(PDA couple in front of me enjoying a romantic evening sprawled out on their blanket at a fireworks display. They are kissing for an obnoxiously prolonged period of time) Please stop kissing each other in front of me and stop doing it with your eyes open, I beg you, please.

(An extremely beautiful man is sitting at the coffee shop with his friend and he is talking about calorie intake and protein. I am surprised by my repulsed reaction, with every minute he talks about work out reps I find it more vomit-inducing than the last minute) I didn't know it was possible to hate someone this beautiful this much.

(Scrolling through Facebook) Oh good, another 18 year old getting engaged. I'm going back to bed. Wake me up when they're divorced in three months.

Meme: You are not alone. You matter.
Me: Uh, yes I am alone and we are all matter.

I'm in a rancorous mood. I think I'll go drive around and blast old school Lil Jon through some nice suburban neighborhoods. In my minivan.

(About to pee in a public restroom and I notice the seat is covered in urine) The person in here before me should have just saved themselves the trouble and peed directly on me.

Me: And most nights I can't even fall asleep because I'm crippled by the fear of never being loved by a man.
Friend: Well, what about Tony? I know he's interested in you.
Me: No, please, just let me die alone.

Ad on the Radio: Are you getting married, buying a house, writing your will?
Me: No and no and yes.

(Scrolling through Facebook) Are people intentionally trying to make their faces look like buttholes when they do that weird, puckered up, duck face thing in pictures?

(Man on the street cat calls me) Dude, what do you think is going to happen when you do that? What kind of reaction are you trying to illicit? Do you honestly think I'm gonna turn around, clutch my pearls, and exclaim, "Oh, the man of my dreams! My knight in shining armor! It's you! It really is you! Let's get married and have loads and loads of babies." Ok, you know what? I am going to start doing that from now on.

If a guy is talking to his friend about his workout regimen loud enough for me to hear, is that an invitation for me to go over there and smack him in the face?

I'm torn between my desire for a significant relationship and my deep loathing for everything that lives and breathes.

Thoughts That Prove I'm Still Trying to Get it Together

(Walks a mile to Walgreens) What did I come here for?

(Begins walking out of the apartment in underwear) Oh pants. That's right, I was gonna wear pants today.

(Checking my bank balance) It's like I'm just begging for financial ruin.

Everyone is getting married and having babies and I'm a 23 year old diagnosed teeth grinder who just wasted $30 on a mouth guard I'll never use because I can't sleep with things in my mouth.

(Flushes toilet, opens stall door, realizes toilet did not flush correctly, turns around for a second and final flush, turns back around to exit, and am struck in the face with the stall door) Yes, of course. Why wouldn't that happen?

(On the third day of not showering, with unkempt hair and marinara sauce spilled down the front of one of my rattiest t-shirts) Did I just get honked at by a truck full of firemen? I stilllllll got it.

My dating life this summer has consisted of seeing hot guys at social functions once in a while and sometimes they see me.

Great. I just sprouted another gray hair. You're 23 and you have three gray hairs, but you don't have a date for Friday night. Gooooooooooood for yewwwwwwww.

I could go out for a bit and socialize with humans or I could stay at home and clip my toenails over the garbage. Let's see what's sitting in my bank account. Hm. Still $5000 in debt. Toenails it is.

That was riveting. I also learned a valuable life lesson that you should never, ever clip your toenails directly after going to the gym. Duly noted.

I think I'll take this time to recall every single stupid and embarrassing mistake I have ever made since I was a child and dwell on them. Ok, you have 7 minutes. I give myself 7 minutes to sulk.

(I walk into my office and notice an empty packet of hot chocolate on the floor) Ok. I know I didn't have that. I don't drink hot chocolate. Somebody is literally breaking into my office and sipping a warm cup of holiday cheer after hours. Why didn't they steal anything?! There's a lot of good stuff in here!! Wait…wait…something's missing. Yup. My hand lotion is gone. YOU TAKE MY HAND LOTION BUT YOU LEAVE THE KEURIG BEHIND? WHO ARE YOU?

Dear Jesus, Please don't let my dress fly up so that everyone can see my 50 cent, comes-in-a-pack-of-8-from-Wal-Mart granny panties. Thanks.

I wonder if other grown women have contemplated the idea of sitting on Santa's lap and asking for a husband. I bet I'd at least get a date with Santa for trying it.

When I was younger, I thought it was cool to spend an exorbitant sum of money on clothing. Now I'm like, "You know what's cool? Going to Wal-Mart and getting a pair of shorts for $4."

(At the grocery store, post-run, wearing spandex shorts. It is imperative that I pick my front wedgie regardless of the fact that two elderly women are

watching me like a hawk) Yeah, so maybe these shorts *are* too short, but at least these old ladies now know I'm not a boy.

I am having way too much fun using this new stain remover on my white down comforter. I can't think of a more enriching way to spend my Saturday evening. Wait a minute...you can't? You are a boring adult. A beige, beige, boring adult. It's sad.

(Sighs whilst doing my banking) You really need to be careful, dear. *(Pauses)* Stop calling yourself "dear".

I haven't even had kids yet and every time I sneeze a liiiiiiittle bit of pee comes out. What is that about?

I better bring a guy home soon or else my mom's really gonna put me on Christian Mingle this time.

When I was a kid, I imagined that by 23 I would be some gorgeous Hollywood starlet getting wined and dined by a silver screen hunk like we were a regular Bogart and Bacall. I did not imagine that I would be duct taping by computer back together at 9 PM on a Saturday.

Is it wrong of me to feel so giddy and vindicated when I'm told how poorly my ex is doing? His life is in the gutter and my life is really taking off! *(I look around myself)* Is it really though? I mean you just spent the last three of hours of your Friday night eating an entire watermelon by yourself and reading Reddit threads about what it's like to be a high-end escort.

There is a middle-aged, semi-passed out drunk man sitting on the train next to me burping rhythmically and I can't tell if this is just an old drunk guy or me looking at a reflection of myself in the mirror.

Being a woman is weird because you go 23 years of your life convinced that you never want kids to wandering the streets of New York asking men you don't know to give you a baby.

(Sighs) Ok, this is bad. This is really bad. This dress is too short for a day this windy. *(For several minutes, I attempt to walk through the blustery wind holding myself together)* Ok, you know what? If my skirt blows up, everyone's just in for a real treat, that's all I gotta say.

Friend: Shannon, let me set you up with my friend, Frank. He's a doctor.
Me: No, thank you. I met a 35 year old bartender the other night who gave me and fourteen other girls his phone number and I think he and I really have a chance at something, so I'm gonna see where that may lead.

(Looks at phone and doesn't know who is texting me. Remembers what I did the night before) Ok, remember last night was you decided to change your contacts' names to characters from Sesame Street purely because you were bored and you thought it'd be funny? Yeah, that was a bad idea.

(Re-watching "Bridesmaids" now that I'm a few years older) It's honestly like a documentary of my life and Kristin Wig is playing me.

My life is starting to feel like a merry-go-round ride that is being operated by that clown from "It". And the ride is just going faster and faster and I've fallen off the pony and now I'm just hanging on the pole flying through the air. And I'm 5. I may look like I'm in my 20's, but inside I'm a 5 year old falling off of the merry-go-round.

Maybe if I put some mascara on it will mask the fact that I haven't brushed my teeth…in four days.

Whoops. Let me get the glob…oh look at that you've smeared it all over your nose. Good job, Shannon. How do you plan on doing anything if you can't even put mascara on without it looking like you just dipped your nose in an ink well?

This is what happens when you buy mascara from a gas station.

Congratulations. You are officially a crack whore.

I guess the morning wouldn't be complete without spilling some of my coffee all over the floor of Starbucks. There goes $4.

...And a little bit on the keyboard of my laptop. Just wipe it off with your coat. Help the environment. Huh. Interesting. By wiping the coffee off my laptop it has swished onto my phone.

That's great, Shannon. You just spilled coffee down your shirt. Why don't you just buy your iced coffee and then pour it all over your head at the counter next time.

Here I am. An annoying Starbucks beatnik doing my obnoxious "I'm a freelance writer who spends $4 on a coffee so I can use the Wi-Fi here for eight hours" and I can hear a girl who is a good five years younger than me talk about her Olympic hockey training and her desire to go to Cornell Law after a sports career. I don't even know what I'm having for lunch. I might not even be having lunch. I can't afford lunch. Or a law degree from Cornell.

Why am I smelling fish in Starbucks? Is that me again?

Well my $5 shirt is definitely stained for life. I think I'll use this as an excuse to justify a $200 shopping spree at Old Navy. I'm dying to wreck my line of credit anyway.

You know, if you stopped buying $4 iced coffees you'd be able to afford a computer that wasn't held together by duct tape.

My skirt has definitely been tucked into my underwear for the last three blocks. Ah. So good. Do I pull it out or just keep walking like I don't care? I don't care.

One of these days I'm going to find out what the word contour means and then I'm going to do it.

Thoughts I've Had When I'm Being Socially Awkward

(Doing three minute wall squats in a boxing class. Everyone is having an uncomfortable time when I decide to pipe up with something useful) "It's like we're all just taking a niiiiiiiice long shite, boys. We're all just taking a niiiiiiiiiiiiiice loooooooooong shite." *(My remark is met with looks of discomfort. I realize what I've done.)* It is exactly comments like these that are the reason why I can't make anything work with a man.

Stop saying "poop" to strangers, Shannon.

10 year old boy to my brother upon seeing me: Who is that?!
Brother: That's my sister.
10 year old boy: I heard your sister likes guys under 5 foot. I'm 4'9 myself.
Me in my head: I gotta hand it to him, that's pretty smooth. I think I'll start using that line when I'm coming on to guys.

Well, to be honest, I didn't realize somebody could see me when I angrily picked my front wedgie but now that I know this I don't care.

If you spent less time telling your dates that you think putting a condom on your hand and offering to scoop patrons' food portions at Chinese buffets is the funniest thing in the world, you'd probably be married by now.

Woman to her friend walking out of the coffee shop: Well, thanks for having coffee with me!
Me: You're welcome.
(Stares from the strangers)
Shannon, why do you do things like this?

Wow, I'm standing around a marble island countertop in the kitchen cutting carrots at a dinner party and talking about how "Carla just had her third kid and the doc tied up her tubes" and "John lost some money in the stock market this morning so he's really bummed about that". Am I a grownup now?

(Surrounded by grownups having a grown up conversation)

Grownup Number 1: I do think it would be a good idea to get the white papers in by next Monday so we can make time for edits.

Grownup Number 2: And CC it to Dave so he can be in the loop on the changes we're making.

Me: And in case anyone is wondering, singing while doing a headstand is exactly as difficult as it sounds.

(As I finish parking my car on the street, something catches my attention) Oh my…holy…hello. There is a beautiful man walking the streets of Jamestown. Well don't just stand there, go after him! No, no. Don't do that. Remember what happened the last time? Oh no, he's looking over here. Why are you still staring at him?! Look away! Ok, well, you blew that.

(Walking to my office, I look out the window and notice the man is still outside) It's a sign. Go to him. Say something. "Do you want to talk to me?" NO! You're not Anna from Frozen. Ok just pretend you left something in your car, walk back outside, and then back into the building. *(I do this. As I return back to the building, he sees me. I see him. I walk INTO THE DOOR NOT THROUGH IT)* Yeah, you blew it again.

Shannon, you honestly have to stop randomly kicking men in the streets. I can't count how many times you've just run up to a guy you barely knew and kicked him just because you thought it would be funny. It's not funny. It's annoying. Stop doing this.

You are the human equivalent of a Chihuahua just going around yipping at people's ankles. You're not going to get people to like you by kicking them. You

should have learned that in preschool.
You're 23 now.

At the rate I'm going there is a statistically high probability that I will be the old lady at buffets who can be spotted stuffing chicken wings in her pant pockets that are lined with plastic bags, smacking the behinds of the entire wait staff, and then leaving.

The guy working at the gas station counter is STRAPPING. What a dreamboat. Don't look him in the eyes, he'll know. He's probably like 17 or something…in which case, jail. Look away! Look away! Ok, now you're just nervous laughing in public. Everyone's staring.

A little less Britney and a little more Princess Diane upon exiting the vehicle, please. Particularly in front of construction workers.

(Sees a beautiful, shirtless man walking down the street. Begins running after him. While sprinting...) What are you doing, Shannon? Do you realize what is happening? You literally just started running after a man because he's pretty. Stop this! Have you no pride? My feet won't stop. My heart says "yes", but my head says, "no". *(Finally reaches him, by this point we are walking side by side and I'm panting. Upon his face is a look of concern. My brain does not register this and I just continue to walk with him, panting and fully maintaining eye contact)* ...there is no explanation for what is wrong with me.

Wow. Going to the bathroom in public with someone in the stall next to me is really awkward. How do I fill these long silences? I wonder if I should say "tickle me" in the Elmo voice to break the tension.

(Running out of coffee shop to move my car and I pass a random guy standing in line at the counter)
Me to him: I'm just gonna run outside real quick and move my car before I get a ticket.
Him:....ok.
My brain: Why do I feel the need to tell complete strangers what I'm doing all the time?

(Standing at the counter of a café waiting for my iced tea. A middle-aged man comes over)
Him: Oh sorry, I didn't mean to invade your space. I was just checking out the muffins.
Me: You're good.
Him: But if I'm being honest, I was checking out your muffins too.
Me: ....

What the…I don't even have a response for that. My muffins? What are my muffins?! Is that my butt? Are my muffins my breasts? My breasts are fully inside my shirt. I'm even wearing a BRA today and I NEVER wear a bra!!!...?????????...What are my muffins?!!! *(30 minutes later)* Maybe he meant my muffin top.

Maybe the next time you hit on a guy you make sure you don't have a piece of chicken wing stuck to the lens of your glasses. And don't do it at 9 AM at the doctor's office.

Old Friend I Hadn't Seen in Years: What about you? Are you seeing anyone?
Me: Uh, well eight months ago an Italian rapper named Flavio bought me a one dollar bracelet from a Somalian immigrant selling them in the streets of Pisa and uh, since then not so much. Oh but then there was this one time two months ago that I

went on a date with a Turkish Muslim and when I ultimately ended up declining his offer to date seriously, he hopped on OK Cupid right in front of me, but not before insulting my weight. Who knew OK Cupid was still a thing? And I learned I was fat that night.

So...I think I'm single. And I know you didn't ask for any of this information, but I feel your life would be richer for knowing it.

Thoughts I've Had That Prove I'm Delusional

(At the movie theater, watching Wonder Woman) Holy crap, all this time and I never realized I was exactly like Wonder Woman. It's like looking in the mirror.

Zac Efron is single. I'm single. Coincidence? I think not.

Anytime I walk down the aisle of a moving train I imagine I look like Angelina Jolie in "The Tourist" where Johnny Depp watches her in awe but actually I look like Frank Gallagher after a bender.

(Walking through a government building filled with law enforcement officials)

Man in a tie: "Good morning".

Me: "Morning." Wow, he said "good morning" to me. I wonder if these people think I'm a cop since I'm wearing my power lesbian suit today. Detective Nixon. That is spicy.

(Staring at myself naked in the mirror) I am a gift to mankind.

There is a very real disconnect between the woman I am and the woman I think I am. In my head I live in a nice brownstone and I meditate on the things that I'm thankful for every morning and drink matcha tea and eat salads out of a mason jar. I HAVE LITERALLY NEVER EATEN A SALAD OUT OF A MASON JAR BEFORE BUT THIS IS WHO I BELIEVE I AM. But the real me can't discern the clean underwear from the dirty underwear strewn about my floor. You know what? Screw it. Stop trying to be something you're not. Be the pig that you are. I'M A PIG.

(Guy walks into the café) I'm so glad I decide to wear a pushup bra today. Not that it matters. You actually need to have something that can be pushed up in order for a pushup bra to work.

(Heading to the gym where a famous actor works out that I have been stalking recently) What do you think is going to happen, Shannon? You're just gonna waltz in there and he's gonna take one look at you and be like, "That the one. That's the girl I'm marrying." Look at yourself right now. You are walking to the train station with an entire hardboiled egg stuffed in your mouth because you didn't make time to cook breakfast. Mind you, you didn't even chew the hardboiled egg, you just sucked it in like a golf ball through a garden hose, you freaky little human chipmunk. You also left home without brushing your hair, shaving your pits, or showering in the last 72 hours. And you HONESTLY believe you have a shot at getting this guy's attention?! You changed nothing about yourself. You have improved yourself in no way. That is some level of arrogance.

Shannon, the reason you're still single is because you spend all of your free time trying to find Jeff Goldblum so you can elaborately propose to him rather than actually dating people in the real world.

Thoughts I've Had as an Insomniac

(Lying in bed at 1 AM) Is French toast just toast in France? And why do we only hear about French toast? Why isn't there Papa New Guinea toast…why are you like this? FALL. ASLEEP.

(2 AM) What if kids were Big Macs and Big Macs were kids? And we raised Big Macs and ate babies.

(2:30 AM) Has anyone made a cold sweat scented perfume? That, I would buy.

(3 AM, finally feeling myself start to fall asleep) My brain: I noticed that you're drifting off. Now seems like a good time to remind you that you're probably going to die alone, watch your younger brothers get married before you, and never make any significant contribution to society. I'M AWAKE. I'M AWAKE!!!!

(4 AM) You'll see people drinking a drink, but you'll never see anyone beveraging a beverage. WHY.

(4:30 AM) I don't know where my gallbladder is or what it is, but I think I need to remove it.

Thoughts I've Had Since First Moving to New York

(Sees a $4.99 clearance rack full of shorts on the street) And if you grab 'em and run, they're $0.00. Heh, heh, heh…my dark side both scares and impresses me at the same time.

One of the great things about living in New York is the complete lack of privacy. Exhibit A: I'm in my apartment and suddenly I notice that I can see inside my neighbor's apartment clear as day and they can see me. And what I saw, I cannot un-see. There, in all his glory, was a man propped up on his lazy boy, spread eagle. Just the most pristine shot of a crotch I've ever seen in my life. No shame. I could see nothing but the waste down. Granted, he was at least wearing boxers, but I'm tickled by the reality that only in New York will you meet your neighbor by his crotch before you meet him by his face. Oy gevalt.

(Overhearing a conversation)
Girl: Yeah my roommate and I just saw that movie last night!
Another Girl: Oh really? My roommate actually just mentioned it to me the other day!
The Third Girl: My roommates and I were planning to go next week.
Me: Wait a minute, it sounds like these people actually hang out with their roommates…almost like they are friends or something. I don't even know what my roommate does for a living. Actually, I haven't seen her in about four days. Do I even have a roommate?

How did I end up on a tiny island in the middle of the East River between Queens and Manhattan?

It's a good thing that you have such unfettered trust in total strangers, Shannon, because otherwise riding a completely empty bus out of Roosevelt Island with nobody but the driver at 1 AM would be really scary.

You never ever see camels around here and I wanna know why that is. Wait a minute, yes I have seen a camel here. I saw a camel sitting outside the David Letterman Show. That's right, camels are here! I amaze myself every day. Here I was this whole time thinking about camels in NYC and I actually have seen a camel in NYC. This town really does have it all. Why are you thinking about this at 2 AM? You need to talk to your doctor about sleeping pills or something. This isn't right.

For the people who wanna know what living in New York is like, it's this in a nutshell: you and your neighbor have seen each other naked through your open windows more than anyone has ever seen you naked in your entire life and the two of you have never spoken a word to each other. Ever.

(In my first weeks of living in NYC, I was amazed by the piles of fresh toilet paper rolls that were in each bathroom) It blows my mind that these establishments will just leave all of this high end toilet paper out here. Aren't they afraid people will steal it? I could stuff about nine rolls in my purse right now and not have to buy any for the apartment for a month…ok Shannon, you are ghetto.

Thoughts I've Had on the Subway

(On the train, in public, I start choking on my food, yet manage to clear my airway before dying) Well, that was embarrassing. And scary. If I hadn't just pooped earlier, I would have pooped my pants.

You know why you started choking, don't you, Shannon? Because you shoved 19 pizza-flavored combos in your mouth without swallowing once.

(Gets into air conditioned subway cart) Yessssss, this is amazing. I should just get out of my lease at the apartment and live out of a subway cart. This thing has air conditioning. My apartment doesn't have air conditioning.

I wonder what it would be like to really live on the subway. Think about it...you could take an entire cart and just convert it into an apartment. How amazing would that be? A moving apartment. One day you wake up in Coney Island and the next you are in Time Square.

Lady who comes onto the subway: Any change you got is change I need. You got change to spare? 'Cuz any change you got is change I need.
Me: Lady, I was just marveling at the idea of living out of a subway cart. Does that shed some light on how poor I am? You're not getting anything from me.

(On the subway) Stop thinking about intersex people and smiling about it, Shannon. Now

that man sitting across from you thinks you were coming on to him.

(I'm on the subway heading to the office and shoving a giant salami sandwich down my throat after my morning workout. An attractive, debonair man enters the subway at the next stop. My entire demeanor changes) Oh get real, Shannon. Don't take such dainty nibbles as if you weren't just inhaling the entire sub in the three bites. There are bread crumbs in your hair. Give it a rest, he already saw you, you forest animal.

Lazy Thoughts

(Disgusted with myself) It is so unbecoming of a lady to willfully spend six consecutive hours binge-watching television. Go do something with your life. Be a productive member of society! *(Gets off the couch, walks to*

the refrigerator, opens the door, stares inside for a second, closes it, returns to the couch) That was pretty good.

There are 15 year old children out there winning Olympic gold medals and I just licked off the marinara sauce that I spilled on my t-shirt. I didn't even rinse out the stain with soap and water, I just licked it. Am I doing something wrong?

The fact that you just considered ordering floss off of Amazon Prime instead of going to the store proves you are a lazy scumbag, Shannon.

Surely you have better things to do on a Saturday afternoon than watch yourself eat a carrot in front of the mirror.

I wonder if anyone else just sits around on their lard backside watching videos of other people working out. These women are inspiring, but they're only inspiring me to continue watching them do their butt-clenching exercises while my butt maintains the consistency of pancake batter…I'll do a squat.

But seriously, it's time to cut the crap and get your life together. And it starts right after you binge the entire series of Shameless on Netflix because you only get 7 days free.

(At the gym) Man, this is hard. *(Glances at the time)* I've been here 6 minutes.

The 12 year old you would not recognize who you are today. That is not a compliment, Shannon.

(Lying on my bed aimlessly) I'm so tired. But I'm hungry. But I'm too tired to get up. But I'm too hungry to go to sleep. I mean how bad is it really to eat a bowl of ice cream at 1 AM? Not bad. I'm a grown up. I can do whatever I want. *(30 minutes later and I haven't moved)* I'm so tired. But I'm so hungry. I should just get up and get the freakin' ice cream. *(Finally succeeds at getting my lard butt out of bed. Back in bed five minutes later with a bowl of ice cream, purring contentedly)* I'm so glad I did this. Eight-hundred calories right before bed was the right decision.

Spotify Ad: "Do you want transform your life? You can do that with sliced almonds! Buy a pack of almonds today from me, celebrity trainer Katie Snowflake." Lady, I just ate four Chaco Tacos for breakfast. I am not your audience.

(Watching reality TV at 3 PM on a Wednesday) I'm basically a housewife without a husband or kids.

(I realize a television show I watch has its season premiere) Dude, I'm so happy! My life has meaning now!!

...ok, did you hear what you just said? What does that tell you about yourself?

Thoughts Regarding my Relationship With Food

I feel bad for pigs not because we kill them for bacon, but because they'll go their whole lives never knowing how great bacon tastes.

I'm roasting marshmallows for breakfast. Rather, I would, if I could find a stick. I wonder if I could just use this fishing pole instead.

I could have a kale smoothie and feel good about myself. Or I could eat an entire chocolate cake and hate myself. I already hate myself, so I should stick with cake.

I've always wanted to die in a really valiant way. Like being assassinated. Yet I'm sure that's not how I'll croak. There is a statistically high likelihood that I will die from choking on a hot dog or something since I'm always throwing food down my open gullet like the greedy, hedonistic, unrestrained Philistine that I am.

I don't even know how people can survive without at least three cups of coffee and two diet cokes a day. One day I just drank water. No coffee. No diet coke. I didn't even make it till 4 pm.

(Eating steak) Mm, dead animals. My favorite.

My coffee tastes exactly like Satan told his St. Bernard Julius to take a massive crap in Miracle-Gro, put it in a K-Cup, and call it Starbucks Mocha flavored coffee.

Ok, Shannon, you are only here to get some kale for your green smoothie. Nothing else. OH KLONDIKE BARS!!! I would do some seriously questionable things for a Klondike bar. NO! You don't need that. The kale smoothie will be just as good. Yeah, right. Ok, get the kale and then just get a candy bar to balance it out. No, that's not healthy enough. But a package of chocolate chip cookies is. Yes, get the cookies.

Honestly, Shannon, can't you wait until you're at least out of the store before you start stuffing cookies in your face? Thank God this is a Tops and not Whole Foods.

These cookies are crispy. Like potato chips. So if I eat like 30 of these, it's not a big deal because they are basically just the dessert version of chips. And you can eat 30 chips.

...I'm puking.

I hate myself.

Ok, one more.

What the heck is this crap? I thought I bought ice cream. This tastes life cat vomit. What's in here? *(Looks at label)* No artificial flavors. Made with cane sugar. Vegan. What the---I picked up healthy ice cream?! I didn't want this garbage! I can actually taste eggs in here! Where are my chemicals?!

I forgot a knife to cut my steak. I could walk three steps to the drawer and grab one. Or I could just shove this entire thing in my mouth. Good. Now I'm choking.

(Eating my 18th chicken wing) Honestly, how I'm gaining weight, I don't know. It's a mystery to me.
The look on my server's face: I could probably tell you why.

Am I the only one who, while at the movies, will just throw a handful of popcorn at my face and hope some of it lands in my mouth?

I feel that if at least 40% of the movie theater popcorn you are eating ends up in your mouth you are doing something right.

Thoughts I've Had in Yoga Class

My yoga pants have a gigantic hole in the crotch. I just bought these so I feel that I need to get my money's worth by wearing them until something really embarrassing happens.

Yoga would be 1,000 times more epic if we were doing it to "The Dark Knight" soundtrack.

This would not be happening right now if I had a nut sack.

Where are the pizza pockets?

Should've worn a bra.

Hey is that my Tinder date???

I remember his profile: business owner, director of a children's orphanage in Kenya, rock-climber, photos of him with dogs and children in third world countries...dude, have you like, ever even been to jail yet? Cuz if you haven't, I'm not interested.

Wow. Nice forearms, Thor.

Should have met him for coffee.

Yeah, I'm definitely not into blondes. Or men who look like they're probably under 40. Or any man in general who has his life together.

PUSHUPS???? This is yoga!!!!

Why do I keep forgetting to start the application process to sell my eggs? I need to do that when I get home.

Please just let me be fat. Why couldn't this be yoga with pizza pockets and donuts class? Or just pizza pockets and donuts class?

Lady, why do you hate us???

Donuts.

Ma butt gon' be so FAAAAAAWYN.

Wow. Look at her butt. I would trade half my rack for a butt like that.

Thoughts I've Had at The Dentist's

(Entering the waiting room) Who are all of these people and why are they here?

(Taking my seat and scanning the premises) You know, I remember waiting rooms before the advent of cell phones. When we would all just intensely stare into space hoping we wouldn't awkwardly make eye contact with

anyone. Oh crap, I just made eye contact with someone. Why aren't you looking at your phone, stupid?

(An uncomfortable, somewhat painful device is placed in my mouth to take photos of my back molars) Things could be worse. It could be in my butt.

Why are they playing two girls one cup music in here? Oh wait, that's Ed Sheeran.

I just want some freakin' chives.

Dental Hygienist: Are you interested in getting your wisdom teeth removed?
Me: Oh yes.

My Brain: Lady, I am lying to you. I didn't get my wisdom teeth taken out five years ago when I was first told I needed to and I won't be doing it now.

Dental Hygienist: And what do you do to maintain the health of your teeth?
Me: I brush my teeth morning and evening, floss daily, do a rinse every few days, and have drastically reduced my sugar intake.
Dental Hygienist: Very good.
My Brain: Another lie. I brush my teeth every four days or when my breath starts to smell like a raccoon crawled into my mouth and died in there.

You don't have to fill these long silences. My boyfriend doesn't even do that. He doesn't even exist.

Gosh, I would just hate a job where I had to touch people's faces all day long. I'd take a job where I'd have to punch people's faces though.

I get that you feel compelled to fill these long silences but I'd hope as a medical professional who went to school for more than half a decade and came out with a degree you would understand the basic logic that I cannot respond to your questions when I have what is essentially a ball gag in my mouth.

Thoughts I've Had on a Blind Date (Round 1)

For $13 I'll stuff this entire breadstick in my mouth.

How long do I have to pretend I'm a grownup before I get to throw the word "poop" into the conversation? POOP!!!!!!!! HAHAHAHAHAHAHA...great. Now I have to poop.

Is it bad form to hit on the waitress during a date? He probably wouldn't even know I'm hitting on her by asking, "So just how much cheese can we get exactly?"

Maybe he'll leave if I ask him to get a vasectomy. Nope, that didn't work.

Why don't we take this back to my place?
(Speaking to my food)

We need to bring the world "cockalorum" back.

How am I going to pick this wedgie without anyone noticing? Perhaps picking it in front of him is my ticket out of here. No. Even better. I'll ask him to pick my wedgie.

Why am I here when I could be at home, naked, licking Cheeto crumbs off my chest whilst binge watching horribly produced television?

You know what was good television? Teletubbies. Teletubbies was just excellent. Those little nitwits were like Barney's gay, British, semi-retarded sperm. Man I loved them. Tinkyyyy winkyyyyyyy. Boy do I feel sorry for the guy whose wife calls his pecker that.

Thoughts I've Hand on a Blind Date (Round 2)

Oh yeah. This feather boa was the right decision. So is this "Frankie Says Relax" t-shirt.

I miss Muppet babies.

This guy is smokin' hawt. Say something to impress him. "I can literally eat 40 pizza rolls in one sitting." Yeah, that wasn't it.

Dude, how much do you bench?! I bet he could crush me like a walnut between a stripper's butt cheeks…you should say that to him.

Give up, Shannon. You are the female Mr. Bean.

I know I just met this guy, but I wonder how pissed he would be if I just ordered a martini and threw it in his face. I've always wanted to do that.

You've gone a really long time without saying any words. I wonder if he's noticed I'm not paying attention.

Thoughts I've Had on a Blind Date (Round 3)

(30 seconds in) Why don't we call it a night?

I have a pair of tweezers in my purse. Would it be so wrong if I just reached across the table and plucked that one hair out of his nose?

It's like it's just staring me in the face, screaming, "Free me, Shannon, free meeeeeee."

IT FELL IN HIS FOOD! OH KILL ME! YOU SPRINKLE CHICKEN PICCATA WITH PARMESAN REGGIANO NOT BODILY HAIRS!!!

The next time I go on one of these things I'm coming with a chastity belt worn on the outside of my pants.

Or I'll just arrive wearing a Batman cape. I'll talk in the Batman voice the entire night. Which, when I do it, really just sounds like Gollum.

I'll wear the belt AND the cape. I'll wrap it around me and tell him it's my cloak of invisibility.

I could be watching Monty Python right now.

Are you suggesting that coconuts migrate?

Don't show me your Pokémon collection. Please. No. What are you doing? You're 30.

This is it. This really is it. I'm gonna die alone.

Four days will pass. I'll have died in my apartment and no one will know and by the time they find me, my cats will already have started eating my face.

Oo, a quarter. Is it weird that I just picked that up while he was still talking?

The Time I Broke My Leg in a Rock-Climbing Accident in Spain and Was Taken in by a Former French Foreign Legionnaire Named Jean Claude

I feel that I have to include this story in the book because it's probably the only good one I have (even though anyone who's ever met me has already heard it at least twice).

I was 21 and in the throes of my solo European backpacking trip that I had to go on to "find myself" or something trite and cliché.

I distinctly recall one afternoon at my hostel in Nice, France sitting 'round the lunch table with a couple of Irish lads that I'd befriended.

Out of the blue, one pipes up with, "What's everyone's coolest scar?"

We showed off what we got and then it was his turn. He pulled up his pant leg a bit and exposed the most pristine, Frankenstein's monster-esque scar I had ever seen. Truly, it was the most astounding piece of work I had seen in my life. I think at one point while my jaw was still dropped, I began to drool.

None of my dinky little scars were even worthy of being in the presence of his mammoth scar. As I looked on in awe, somewhere in the subconscious layer of my mind, I thought, "I gotta get me one of those".

So I did.

After my stint in Nice, I packed up my bags and traveled off to Barcelona, Spain.

While there, a group of new friends I'd met at the hostel (and one Austrian stalker who followed me from France to Spain because he was "falling in love" with me) decided to spend the day at an indoor rock-climbing gym. I had never been to one before, but I had been itching to get into climbing.

So we all went, grabbed some climbing shoes, and hit the bouldering walls. It didn't take long for my adrenaline to start pumping and I always think I'm more gifted at things than I really am. There wasn't a moment that I stopped to rest. I'd scurry up the bouldering wall, get to the top, and climb up over the wall to the little platform that you could walk on to get to the stairs. I must have done this close to ten times before I started to become fatigued. But even once the exhaustion kicked in, I ignored it.

On my final ascent, I reached for the last hold at the top of the wall and my sweaty hand couldn't maintain a strong grip. I slipped and fell about twenty feet, which is a long enough distance for you to think a four letter word in your head as you are going down.

I plummeted to the bottom and when my feet hit the ground I hear a loud pop come from my left ankle. I looked up at my friends. Their faces were white. I refused to look at my foot for fear that my bone was sticking out.

"D'ja hear that?" I asked, with warped enthusiasm. "My bone popped."

"Yeah, we heard that," one of the boys said, with horror in his eyes.

"Ya wanna set my bone back in place?" I inquired, casually.

"No, I can't do that," said the boy, still in a bit of shock. "Let's see if you can walk on it."

The boys picked me up and tried to hold me steady as I attempted to take a step. I couldn't even put weight on my foot.

They carried me to the sofa in a separate room in the gym.

"That's not looking too good," said the Austrian, as my foot steadily began to balloon up.

"Probably sprained it," I said as the pain began to worsen.

"We should get you to a hospital."

"Nah, it'll be good in a few minutes. Just let me ice it." After several minutes of icing my foot, the pain and swelling severely increased. I couldn't argue it any longer. I had to go to a hospital.

We asked the manager of the gym where the closest hospital was and he gave us directions to a nearby clinic.

I have no idea why, but we didn't bother calling a cab. I just propped my arms up on the boys' shoulders and they helped me hobble along half a mile to the clinic.

As soon as we arrived there, I was asked for my passport, which miraculously I did have on me. I handed it over and after looking at it, I was told I couldn't be seen by that clinic but there was another one across town that would be able to examine foreigners like me.

"Screw it," I said. "Let's just go back to the hostel. I'm tired and it's already starting to feel better, so I'm sure I don't even need to be looked at."

Apprehensively, the boys honored my request and we called a cab back to the hostel.

One of the boys was kind enough to run to the pharmacy to buy me some crutches and I rested on my bed while I waited for him to come back.

While in the dorm, a girl from Texas saw my cantaloupe sized foot and asked what happened. When I told her I figured I'd just sprained my ankle and would be better in the morning, she shook her head.

"That's not a sprain. I broke my foot six months ago and it looked exactly like that," said Daisy (Daisy isn't her real name, but I forgot her real name so from now on the Texan girl is Daisy). "You really should go to the hospital. I'll go with you."

Daisy and I hopped in another cab and drove to the clinic that would actually see me. As soon as we got there, they asked for my passport. I reached for it in my purse. It wasn't there.

"I left it at the other clinic," I told Daisy. So she walked and I hobbled back to the other clinic, retrieved my passport, and headed back to the clinic we started at.

"Wait a minute, how much is this gonna cost?" I asked the woman at the front desk, remembering I was in a foreign country and didn't have health insurance.

"For the visit it is 100 euros and you will also need x-rays."

"X-rays?! Well, how much will that cost?"

"18 euros."

Daisy and I looked at each other impressed. Obviously, coming from the United States there is no such thing as x-rays for 18 euros. It was a sweet deal, so I agreed to the x-rays even though it was starting to look like I had no choice anyway.

As we sat in the waiting room, I could tell Daisy was getting antsy. She had an early flight to Rome in the morning and hadn't even started packing.

"Just go back to the hostel. You've done enough for me already. I'm sure they'll look at it and tell me it's just a sprain. Then I'll call a cab and come right back to the hostel."

After enough coaxing, Daisy agreed to leave me behind.

Soon after, I was taken in for my x-rays and soon after that the doctor returned with the results.

"How is it, doc?"

"Very bad."

Those were not the words I wanted to hear.

"Oh? How bad?"

"We can't treat you here. You will need to go to another hospital. You're going to need surgery."

Reality was not hitting me.

"Can't I just leave?"

"No, this is an emergency. You absolutely need your foot taken care of. We will call an ambulance and get you to the hospital right away."

I can't say any of this really frightened me. I was mostly just irritated.

Within minutes, an ambulance arrived and the EMTs brought in a gurney. They strapped me into it and started wheeling me out the front door, but not before the lady at the front desk said, "Wait, you forgot to pay!"

I whipped out my credit card, handed it to an EMT, the EMT handed it to the lady, and the lady ran it through the machine.

By the grace of God, the clinic's machine was broken. They let me go without paying the 118 euros.

For the record, riding in an ambulance strapped on a gurney in a foreign city where you are all alone is not as fun as it sounds. And it just kept getting worse.

They wheeled me into the hospital and plopped me down on one of the hospital beds. I was in a room surrounded by what I can only describe as a bunch of dying, old people.

The woman in the bed next to mine was in excruciating pain. She kept wailing and crying out to me in Spanish. I wish I could say that this is the time that I shared a tender moment with a sick, dying woman and I was consumed with unbridled sympathy and sadness but all I could think was, "Lady, you better not accidentally knock your piss pan over so that it lands on me."

Yes, that is correct. Her pee pot was just sitting up on her bed in between her legs. Why? I have no idea. To my left was a curtain that divided me from some of the other hospital patients and on that curtain was what I can only imagine to be human fecal matter.

"Like heck I'm gettin' cut open in this joint," I said to myself.

I reached for the crutches beside me, wormed myself off of the bed, and attempted to hobble away.

The nurses yelled something to me in Spanish about not leaving.

I asked them if they spoke English. One told me she spoke a little. I asked if anyone else in the hospital spoke fluent English. She told me that an administrative staff member did and that she would retrieve him.

An hour later Mr. Administrative Man came to me and I peppered him with questions.

"Look, tell me straight, how bad is my foot really?"

"The doctors still haven't been able to look at the x-rays that have been sent over yet, so I couldn't tell you."

"I've been here for two hours now and no one has checked it out yet. They say I might need surgery. When would they do that?"

"Maybe tomorrow at the earliest."

"What? Am I expected to stay here over night?"

"Yes."

"Look, I'm supposed to be on a flight headed to Granada tomorrow morning. I don't want to miss that. And in Granada, I have someone there who can translate for me. I don't have anywhere here. Can't you just do me a favor and clear me? I promise I'll go to a hospital in Granada right away."

The dude must have seen it in my eyes that I wouldn't let this one go. He agreed to let me leave the hospital and I hobbled outside where I awaited a cab to take me back to the hostel.

That ain't the first time I've talked myself out of a hospital stay before. I narrowly escaped the looney bin just six months prior, if you can believe it. But that's a totally different story, we're not talking about that now. We're talking about this.

When I got back to the hostel, I collapsed into a chair in the common area.

My boy friends found me and attentively brought me ice, made me dinner, and got me whatever I needed to feel comfortable.

After fourteen hours of hopping back and forth across Barcelona with a maimed foot that was beginning to feel like it was on fire, I looked around and thought I was the luckiest girl in the world.

I had a sweet, doe-eye, poetic looking British boy help me up the stairs, French-Egyptian sisters keep me company, and nice Spanish people who made sure I got fed. Maybe I was just delirious, but I remember being euphorically happy.

I didn't sleep at all that night. I sat up in bed and waited for the sun to rise. I couldn't wait to get on a plane and go to Granada where I had someone waiting for me and I wouldn't be as alone.

When I arrived at the airport, I was at the mercy of strangers. I just had to hope that as soon as I got out of the cab, someone who see me on my crutches trying to wheel a suitcase and carry a backpack. Fortunately somebody did and pointed me to an area where I could get wheelchair service. I was being wheeled by an abrasive, but protective

Spanish woman who got miffed any time people wouldn't instantly move out of our way or take note that I was crippled. I loved her.

The flight from Barcelona to Granada was short and I remember how doting the flight attendants were.

I got a cab from the Granada airport to a flat in the city center where I was staying.

After being dropped off, I crutched to the door, picked up a flower pot, grabbed the key underneath it, and unlocked the door.

Finally.

The only person I knew well enough to ask for help in all of Spain was a man named Jean Claude, a former French Foreign Legionnaire. I cannot make this up.

I knew Jean from a previous trip and I had met him at the very hostel I was staying at in Barcelona several months earlier.

Interesting fellow. Born in third world communist Venezuela, he left when he was 20 years old to tried to make a life for himself in Europe. Between homelessness and odd jobs, he ended up in the French Foreign Legion in his mid-20's. Afterward, he established himself in Granada, Spain. Since then, he had been working as a tour guide while finishing his third masters' degree or something weird like that.

He wasn't home when I arrived at his apartment. But an hour later he came in to find me sprawled out dramatically on his couch, fatigued and famished.

Unamused, he looks at me. "Ah, a woman." he said as he went to hang up his coat.

I grimaced.

"You want to 'splain to me how thees happen?" he inquired, pulling up a chair closer to the sofa.

"I was rock-climbing."

"I know. You told me. And where deed you get thees idea from?"

"From myself," I replied, indignantly.

"Really? There's not some guy you know who does it and you wanted to try it too?"

"Oh don't flatter yourself!" I shot back. "You think you're the inspiration for everything I do? I've wanted to climb long before I met you, I just decided to finally do it."

"Uh huh. Sure. Now, who were you with? Climbers? Or stupid kids who don't know what they're doing?"

"Some people."

"Ok, that answers my question."

"Do you think they're gonna have to amputate it?" I asked.

He examines my foot.

"Mm. Probably." I look at him with terror in my eyes. He continues, "What does amputate mean?"

"To cut off!" I shouted.

"Oh. Maybe. It's too late at night to go to the hospital now, but we will go first thing in the morning. You need to rest. Bedroom is upstairs."

It was apparent that Jean had no plans to help me up the stairs and as I started to hobble up the marble steps on my crutches, he stopped me.

"Hey, wait a minute. Can you carry this upstairs for me?" he asks, holding a mop and a bucket.

"Piss off."

He laughs.

I spent another sleepless night waiting for the sun to come up because the pain was too intense for me to sleep comfortably.

The next morning, Jean and I trekked to the hospital where I was told to take a number and wait until it was my turn to be seen. Four hours later, I was moved from one waiting room to a slightly more intense waiting room. In that waiting room, everyone was sick and dying, kinda like the room I was in when I was at the hospital in Barcelona.

My foot felt as though somebody poured gasoline all over it and lit a match and all I could do was watch my foot go up in flames.

I begged for pain meds. I never got them. I went to take a sip of my water and they slapped it out of my hand. I wasn't allowed to drink anything in case surgery was needed.

Jean had left me briefly and when he came back, I had never been so happy to see another human in all of my life. As they started to wheel me away to the x-ray room, I grabbed his hand and ordered him not to leave me.

We went off to the x-ray room and got new pictures of the injury. Throughout the entire waiting period, I was certain that they would tell me they'd be lobbing off my foot. When the doctor came back and reported that I had a fracture, I nearly kissed him right on the mouth.

"So you won't be cutting it off then?"

"No," he said, giving me a weird look. "We will either put you in a cast or do surgery. We are still trying to figure out if your foot needs it. If we do surgery, we won't be able to fit you in for another three days and you will not be able to leave the hospital until after the surgery."

The idea of being trapped in a hospital for three days did not sit well with me. When they told me I would only be needing a cast, I was ecstatic.

After a full day at the hospital, Jean wheeled me out to the cab with my freshly, white cast and a fat, throbbing foot underneath it.

I spent three weeks living at Jean Claude's humble abode in what is arguably my favorite city in the world.

Although I was crippled during my time in Granada, it is one of the most special memories I have.

If you have never been, I highly suggest it. The climate is tropical and the

Mediterranean Sea is only a 45 minute drive away, but when you are walking the streets of the city center you can see the snowy mountain tops of the Sierra Nevada region. There is a heavy Arabic influence throughout the city and the architectural integrity of the buildings and the romantic cobblestone streets make Granada a quintessentially bohemian fairytale wonderland.

Jean and I would have horrific fights with each other. On two occasions I threw things at him. The first time, I threw my wallet. The second time, I threw my glasses. We just fought about ridiculous things. Sometimes I was miserable, but even through the misery, being in Granada was one of the most beautiful things that has ever happened to me.

After three weeks, it was time for me to return to America. The day I was leaving was bittersweet one. Though Jean and I had violent tempers and routinely clashed with each other, I must acquiesce that I had fallen in love with him (Stockholm syndrome). And at the very least, I think he grew fond of me. He nicknamed me Mallory after Mallory from "Natural Born Killers".

But fondness was not enough; we had too many barriers: language, cultural, distance, and age, among others. Nothing real could have transpired. I was happy to be going home, but I was sad to leave Granada and my captor. The morning before I had to go to the airport, I had to first visit the doctor for a checkup. Jean and I drove to the hospital and consulted with the doctor. She informed us that after taking another round of x-rays, they could see the bone was not healing correctly and that when I returned to the United States, I would need surgery (I had the surgery and got the lovely plate, five pins, and massive scar that I always wanted).

After the trip to the hospital, I spent my last hours at Jeans' flat, counting down the minutes before I would have to call a taxi.

We sat in comfortable silence. I watched him as he maintained a steady gaze straight ahead. He was thinking about something.

"Are you sad that I'm leaving?" I taunted, sarcastically, reflecting on the hellish turmoil we had put each other through.

"Yes," he responded.

I knew he was serious when I could see his eyes had watered up, which only made me have to fight back tears myself.

Jean accompanied me to the airport and we said our goodbyes and I do wish I could say we left it at that---a sweet ending to our short-lived tryst before parting ways and going on with our separate lives. But that's not how real life works.

We wrote to each other every morning and every night for nine months until we arranged a time for me to return to Granada. We tried to make it work, but we were quickly reminded of how much we hated one another so I packed my bags, told him never to speak to me again, and I left. I have since never heard from him again. Good.

The End.

The Doctor, The Pitbull, And The Girl Who Snuck Into a Fashion Show

I used to do this thing where I would randomly respond to sketchy Craigslist ads for modeling gigs, not think twice about it, and just show up at the location where the shoot would take place. One time that location ended up being a hotel.

The whole reason I got myself into this particular situation is because I was sickened by how lazy I had become. You see, I was 19 years old and doing lots of weird things to make money. One time, I pet sat for a lady doctor on the Upper West Side of Manhattan. She paid me $400 to sit in her fancy, $3000 a month doctor lady apartment, hang out with her dog, and do whatever I wanted to for a week.

And it was not good what I did. In one week, I turned into the lazy version of Tom Hanks in "Castaway". Every day I would wake up to a pit bull's butt in my face (the dog couldn't sleep alone). Then the dog and I would cross the street and go for a walk in the park. After that, I'd come back to the apartment, order take out, and watch copious amounts of Frasier episodes over and over again.

On the fifth day, I took a long, hard look at myself; just a giant blob of filth with empty Chinese cartons strewn about the apartment and my waistline expanding.

"You are in one of the greatest cities in the world and this is how you choose to spend your time? This speaks volumes about your character," I thought.

"Go on an adventure," I ordered myself.

So I got on Craigslist.

I linked up with a photographer who told me he was shooting a show for Fashion Week and had some time before the event to do a quick session. I met him at a hotel in midtown Manhattan. We shook hands, exchanged pleasantries, and took a few shots throughout portions of the hotel. See? Not as risqué as I made it sound. After we got our shots, he said, "Well I have to go shoot this show now. You're more than welcome to stay and watch a bit of it. If anyone asks, just say you are my assistant."

I'm a real go-with-the-flow-kind of gal so I just shrugged my shoulders and tagged along. After all, I'd never been to a fashion show before, much less one during Fashion Week in NYC. He set up his camera and then set up a camera in front of me.

"Just pretend you are taking pictures," he instructed.

So there I was, among the throng of professional photographers and the press, just hangin' out waitin' for the show to begin.

It was an experience. I don't get why fashion shows are such a big deal. Everyone is uptight and thinks they're curing cancer as 85 pound girls with knobby knees, bruised legs, and faces that reveal they're dead inside stumble down the runway like Bambi after shooting up heroin. And of course they are all wearing clothing that looks like it was sown together by Helen Keller and thrown up on by Courtney Love.

The moral of the story is…don't hop on Craigslist and respond to modeling ads. They don't all end up the way it did for me (you know, coming out alive and not getting turned into a skinsuit). I've since sobered up a bit with age and no longer do this sort of thing.

Impromptu Hitchhiking

It was some uninspiring day back in April, I don't remember which one exactly. Or maybe it was March. Who knows and who cares. Anyway, all I remember is that it was early spring and I was at the train station in Poughkeepsie, NY awaiting a train to Buffalo. I was going back home for a few days to visit my family. My train was set to depart at 11:53 AM and I was running so late that I was certain I would miss it.

My foot hit the asphalt pavement of the parking lot at 11:51 AM and I dragged my oversized, overstuffed suitcase out of the car and up a couple flights of stairs. I was so desperate to get to the train on time that my belongings were literally flying out of my suitcase and I just kept going because I thought there wasn't time to go back to retrieve everything. Huffing and puffing, I finally made it to the platform and was relieved to discover the train had not yet arrived. After a few minutes of awkwardly standing around and making small talk with others who were awaiting the same train, we all began to develop a sense of agitation. So what if the train was three minutes late? But twelve? One man went to the information desk and came back noticeably irate. Another woman told me she overheard that there was a derailment at Penn Station and that's why the train was late.

"Well do they know when our train is coming here?" I asked.

"I guess that's why the man is mad. The lady at the counter didn't seem to give him any straight answers," explained the woman.

The beast within me had awakened.

"Oh, I'll get us some answers," I huffed as I marched toward the information desk in a state of fury.

As soon as I was in front of this woman who did not deserve her salary, nor did she deserve any working wage because I am a firm believer in actually working for your wages and all she did was sit there arrogantly and uselessly as she might. If you couldn't already tell, I have great distaste for this woman. And I hope she gets fired someday soon.

I slammed by whole body into the counter in a dramatic fashion.

"So what's the deal, huh?" I barked, my face inches from the glass that separated us.

She looked at me trying her hardest not to roll her eyes as I tried my hardest not to Hulk punch the glass window and physically accost her the way Jack Nicholson might accost someone circa "One Flew Over The Cuckoo's Nest".

"You wanna tell us what's going on? Because you got fifteen people standin' outside wondering when the train is comin'."

"You gotta call Amtrak," was all her profoundly useless being could muster up.

"Why would I call Amtrak when you are sitting right here in front of my face? Now,

I heard there was a derailment at Penn Station and that's why the train is late. Is that true?"

"You gotta call Amtrak."

By this point I wanted to strangle this human version of a parrot. But she is dumber than a parrot so that's a bad comparison.

"Why do you work here? Do you serve any purpose or do you just get paid to sit on your butt, regurgitate the same useless words, and roll your eyes at people?"

I was so proud of myself, but honestly I would have felt more fulfilled if there wasn't a thick glass window separating us and I had the ability to reach across the desk, grab her by her weave, and bounce her ugly head off the wall a few times.

"Ma'am, there is nothing I can do."

"That's obvious. What do you suggest I do if this is the sole means of transportation I had relied on to get me from point A to point B today?"

"I don't know."

"Of course you don't."

Oo, she makes my blood boil even today as I write this. She is a useless slug. A plague upon humanity. I wish her forty years of hard labor on a Brazilian cocoa plantation.

I gave up. There was no sense in going to jail over hitting this woman. I retired to the bench and begin complaining loud enough for everyone to hear.

"I'm supposed to be in Buffalo tonight. *Tonight, this very night,* I'm supposed to be in BUFFALO!" I yammer.

Sitting next to me was a zen truck-driver, potentially lesbian woman who was quietly eating her breakfast sandwich.

"Well, if the train doesn't come within 15 minutes I'm just gonna drive to Buffalo. I have a car here. I usually take the train because I live in Buffalo on the weekends but work here in Poughkeepsie during the week. If you want, you can ride with me," this complete stranger offers.

I look at her. I look at her for a few seconds longer. I assess my thoughts on her.

"Yeah, alright, you seem legit," I say, nonchalantly.

So I throw my suitcase in the trunk, hop in the passenger seat, and off I go with madam truck driver. Now, I know what you are thinking. How could a grown woman be so foolish as to voluntarily get in a complete stranger's car and just commit to a five hour journey with them? And I will tell you, this is not the first time I've pulled a stunt like this. About six months earlier I hitchhiked in Ireland after some nice lady offered a ride from the airport to the train station and the girlfriend I was traveling with and I just sat in the back seat giggling about the heart attacks our parents would have if they knew what we were doing.

The first few minutes of my hitchhiking journey were awkward as they generally are whenever you are hitchhiking. But by the end of it, I was friends with this woman even though her name eludes me.

I so wish I could have seen the look on my girlfriend Kym's face when I called her and told her what I was doing. She was none too pleased.

There definitely were a handful of moments throughout the trip when I worried about the truck driver lady's driving skills as she would routinely ride the bumper of every car in front of us. Lesbians. So aggressive. And whenever we would stop off at a rest stop for food and a piss I'd wipe as fast as I could and sprint back outside to the car for fear that she would just take off and leave me in the middle of nowhere.

Anyway, like responding to Craigslist ads for modeling gigs, I can't highly recommend hitchhiking. I suggest erring on the side of caution and finding some alternative means of transporting yourself. I just seem to have dumb luck with these sorts of things.

The Flavio/Fabio Italian Love Triangle

What is Italy without perverse amounts of pizza, gelato, and a spattering of Italian men vying for your affection?

After enduring the unseemly, dreary weather that comes with Octobers in Edinburgh, my travel companion Adriana and I journeyed to Pisa, Italy to soak in the warm, Tuscan sun.

After settling into our hostel, we tossed off our bulky winter coats and adorned ourselves in our flowery summer dresses.

"We have to go out since it's our first night here!" we clamored.

A regular Marilyn Monroe and Audrey Hepburn, we were.

"It is my goal to have three suitors by the end of the week," I announced, astutely, like

I was some loose, modern day Jane Austen character.

Be careful what you set out to do, because it is truly amazing what the human mind is capable of conjuring up.

We freshened ourselves and stepped outside to wander the brightly lit streets of Pisa. Eventually we came across a bustling center known as Garibaldi Square.

We got a table outside of a trendy little restaurant with a young crowd and as my friend swooned over the outrageously thick eyelashes of our pretty male waiter, I was scoping out the area.

I spent a hearty 10 minutes checking out some notably chiseled Italian fellow before realizing he was gay and on a date with his lover.

"Well, that won't work," I conceded.

But beyond him was another character; one far less refined than the beautiful homosexual I had been eyeballing. If someone from The Godfather bred with someone from Jersey Shore…that was this guy. There was an unabashed staring contest that took place for a good hour before I finally started getting nervous.

All of this time, the love child of Michael Corleone and Snooki was watching me. Then he and his friends leaned in and said something to each other. Then the friends started looking our way. One got up, paced around while he took a call, and came back to the table.

It occurred to me what was happening.

"They are human traffickers," I gasped. "We are about to get human trafficked."

I ignored my better judgement and instead of leaving the vicinity, I continued to sit there and keep these thoughts to myself. Eventually, I assured myself that the notion that these boys were human traffickers was a silly one indeed. I decided I would call the boys over.

With a slight tilt of the chin, raise of the brow, and lift of my finger I instructed the Italian gentlemen to join us out our table.

They seemed to get it because they sauntered over.

"Won't you sit down," I ordered, coyly, as if I had been transported to the 40's and was some hot dame like Vivienne Leigh. It is impressive the level of delusion I will attain when I am intoxicated by the realization that I'm in a foreign country.

As the two Italians seated themselves, I initiated small talk.

"What do you do?"

"Guess," said the Godfather/Jersey Shore Italian.

"Human trafficker," I guessed, without missing a beat.

Adriana gasped. "Shannon!"

Godfather/Jersey Shore laughed and when his friend, who spoke no English, inquired why he was laughing, Godfather/Jersey Shore told him in Italian and the non-

English speaking Italian's eye widened and he shook his head vehemently.

"We are in the army," explained Godfather/Jersey Shore.

Figures. I'm always going for military men.

"Oh?" I ask.

"We are paratroopers."

Very good.

"But I'm also a rapper," continued Godfather/Jersey Shore.

Any attraction I might have had for this fellow nearly vanished. Italian soldier who jumps out of airplanes? That's just fine. Guido rapper? No.

"My name is Flavio," the Italian rapper then went on to say.

This guy was just making it worse for himself. I hadn't ever heard the name Flavio before and I didn't like it. Fortunately for him, I have incredibly low standards.

We spent the remainder of the evening having a gay old time with the boys and they even bought us roses. Smooth. When it came time to part ways, we all decided we would meet at the same square the next day so that we could be taken to the Leaning Tower of Pisa.

For that long weekend, I let Flavio the Guido rapper court me.

Several days later, I remained in Pisa to continue my romance and Adriana embarked on an Austrian adventure to visit a friend.

While in Pisa, I befriend a lovely British lesbian named Em who wore a track suit straight out of the 1980's with a messy side ponytail and looked as British as this sentence sounds. We strolled around Pisa and ended up, once again, at Garibaldi Square. As Em and I sat there speaking in English, some boys at the table next to hours interrupted us. They claimed they needed help studying for their English test, overheard us speak English, and asked if they could talk to us to brush up on this new language. Sure, ok.

We allowed them to join us.

"What is your name?" I asked the one boy.

"My name is Fabio."

"And what do you do?"

"I'm a paratrooper in the army."

I was tickled.

"I know someone in the army. He lives in the barracks here. Do you know Flavio?"

Fabio laughed.

"I know Flavio," Fabio confirmed.

"What a small town," I mused.

We all chatted a bit before some of their female cousins joined us and we all had a delightful late afternoon.

As our evening came to a close, Fabio asked what I would be doing the next day. When I told him nothing in particular, he invited me to join him and what I assumed would be the same group of people for an evening out. I agreed. When I met him the next evening at a local restaurant, I quickly realized that it would only be the two of us.

This was a date. And this date I was on, was with a gentleman who spoke very poor, broken English and I spoke no Italian.

For two hours, I politely sat through this awkward event and did most of the talking. I always assume the role of entertainer in uncomfortable situations and talked a mile a minute. Many words I'm sure he did not understand, judging by the quizzical look on his face.

At the end of the evening, he walked me back to my hostel, I said "goodnight", and sent him on his way.

As soon as Fabio departed, I got a message from Flavio. He asked to see me the next day. I obliged. While I was spending a late afternoon with Flavio, I received a messaged from Fabio. Fabio asked, "Are you with Flavio?" And it was at that point, I realized just how ridiculous all of this had become. The good news is that I had a flight to England in the morning so the Flavio/Fabio love triangle could die a natural death. Or death by Shannon fleeing the country.

The real kicker of the story was learning that Flavio had a girlfriend in the next town over that he failed to tell me about. Typical.

The Cop And The Crack Whore

If you think I'm impetuous now, you should have seen me at 19.

When I had set my mind to do something, no matter how stupid it was, there was no stopping me.

A year earlier, I'd bought my first vehicle: a rusty blue Ford Ranger with skull heads for door locks and a skull steering wheel. It is exactly for the skulls and no other reason that I sunk two thousand dollars into this traveling pile of garbage on wheels. Needless to say, after less than a year of driving it and an additional one thousand dollars invested into repairs, it was time for my truck to retire.

At 19, I was wiser (so I believed) and I was going to do the car buying thing the right way. And for the first half of it, I did a pretty good job. I contacted an auto mechanic friend and asked him to help me find a decent, used car. He referred me to a friend and fellow mechanic who he trusted, showed me a few cars, and eventually I settled on a white 1999 Pontiac Grand Am.

I agreed to buy the car and arranged to meet the seller one evening to make the exchange.

Because this garage was out in the boonies and I was driving an old clunker that would either break down or explode at any moment, I invited my friend Katie (bless her, poor dear), to join me on this little adventure. So there we were, a regular Thelma and Louise bouncing around on the back roads of the boonies hitting pothole after pothole and occasionally getting stuck in a mud pit.

"Ok, tell me where we are going," I instructed to Katie as I threw a crumpled piece of paper at her.

"What is this?" she asked, opening it up.

"Directions."

Katie was not very happy with me for writing the directions to this auto garage on an old, crinkled piece of paper colored on and gifted to me by a five year old. Because of the bright crayon colors and my chicken scratch, my navigator had a heck of a time reading out the directions to me. Especially since it was pitch black outside and naturally my old truck didn't have any lights in it.

We made several wrong turns down unsavory areas until we reached the garage.

"Ok here's the money. And here's my piece of crap," I told the mechanic as soon as we reached the garage.

"Do you have the plates?" asked the mechanic.

"What are you talking about?" I asked, puzzled.

"Well, technically, since you are buying this car you need new license plates for it. Look, there are no plates on it now."

"Oooo, I didn't know that."

The mechanic look concerned.

"This isn't exactly legal but I guess this is the only thing we can do at this hour," he said, unscrewing the plates from my Ford Ranger and screwing them onto my new Pontiac Grand Am. "First thing in the morning, take the car to the DMV to get the proper plates and get rid of these ones. Did you get the car registered and insured?"

I looked at him like he had just spoken to me in Klingon.

"Of course you didn't," he said with a sigh. "Well, you're gonna need to do that tomorrow morning too." He finished screwing on the old plates to my new car. "Go home right away tonight and the DMV tomorrow morning. Got it? Don't do anything else before going to the DMV and getting this taken care of."

"Got it," I nodded.

As Katie and I began to leave, I remembered something.

"Oh wait a minute, I got a crap ton of garbage in the back of that truck. Let me take care of that."

And instead of throwing away the garbage like a clean, normal person, I took piles of old fast food wrappers, bags, random scraps of paper, and water bottles and dumped every last piece of trash into the backseat of my new car. I can't even go two minutes of owning a new piece of property without destroying it.

"Ok, good. Thanks. See ya later, Frank."

"Go to the DMV!" I heard the mechanic shout as I peeled off in my new set of wheels.

As you might have guessed, I neither went home that night nor to the DMV first thing in the morning. At this time in my life I was temporarily displaced; meaning I was sleeping under a desk in the office of an old church (don't ask why). The morning after buying my car, I woke up at the butt crack of dawn to go to work and work was a horse farm.

Understandably, since the only living creatures who inhabited my work environment were animals, I couldn't be bothered to gussy myself up. It's not a corporate job; I was scooping dung for a living. After a relatively sleepless night under a desk, I roll out of bed...or more literally rolled out from underneath the desk, put on my jeans, grabbed my Carhartt and trudged out the door in my oversized work boots. That was it. No brushing my teeth. No brushing my hair or washing my face. No changing of the undergarments. Just jeans, boots, jackets, go.

Sure, the mechanic told me to go to the DMV straight away. But I also had to work. So I reasoned with myself that going to work and then going to the DMV was acceptable.

I was just about to pull off the interstate, when in the rearview mirror of my car, I spotted flashing lights. It was happening.

I pulled over. The state trooper pulled over. I sat in my car. He walked toward my car.

"License and registration."

Oo…..yeah. I didn't have that.

"Sir, I have my license and I can give that to you right now. And I have the registration for my old car, but not for this one. I just bought this car last night and I was going to the DMV right after work to get everything taken care of."

The cop didn't care.

"You know why I pulled you over?"

You would think I would have known, but I was the dumbest 19 year old in the world, so I didn't.

"You have the wrong plates on this car. There is also no inspection sticker on it, it's not registered, and it isn't insured."

"Right, but I'm going to do all of that right after work."

"Ma'am, I'm going to have to ask you to step out of the vehicle."

Ah, the glory days. Back when I was 19, I was so naïve. Like Bambi's retarded cousin who had been born to siblings in Virginia and whose mother smoked crack throughout the entire pregnancy. I didn't know I didn't have to oblige the officer, but it's probably a good thing I did. I obviously also didn't know there was a specific process to buying a vehicle (the first time I bought a car, my dad helped me and this isn't something they teach you in high school). At 19, I also wasn't aware of the reality that some cops are straight up douchebags and you sir, wherever you are, whoever you are if you are reading this and I hope you are but I doubt it, you are a douchebag. You are a power hungry, teeny wienie, bully-from-high school, secretly-gay, trapped-in-a-bad-marriage-and-taking-it-out-on-little-girls-who-look-like-crack-whores douchebag (no disrespect to the other blue lives who aren't douches).

Of course, I broke the law. Of course, I was in the wrong. BUT, this cop also went on a power trip. And this is why:

After asking me to step out of the car, he made a phone call.

"Ma'am, do you have any drugs or weapons in the vehicle?"

My eyes widened. In hindsight, it makes sense why he asked that. My crack whore hair was wildly unkempt and was fit for a place in which rats could dwell. I was driving what was building up to look like a stolen vehicle, and within that "stolen vehicle" was a mountain of garbage in the back seat.

"No, I don't have any drugs or weapons," I responded, feeling shaky and nervous.

"Are you sure about that?"

"P-p-p-pretty sure," I stuttered. He looked at me with his stern, repressed homosexual eyes. "I mean, yes," I gulped.

He wouldn't let me get back in the car. A few minutes later, another state trooper pulled up and out came the dogs. That is correct, they brought in the dogs just for me.

"Ma'am, do we have permission to search this vehicle?" asks the trooper.

Again, I didn't know I was legally allowed to tell him to shove it….I mean, to tell him "no".

Shaking, stuttering, and welling up, I just nodded.

There I was. On the side of the road on I-86, with two state troopers, a couple of dogs, and my "stolen vehicle". That was a bad day.

When the dogs couldn't sniff out any of my drugs or weapons, the trooper told me I could get back in the car. He handed me four tickets and told me to leave.

I now know how to properly purchase a car.

Taco Michael

I don't remember where I was coming from or where I was going next. Probably home. It was just after dusk as I hopped off the train stop near my apartment. I spotted a properly Irish establishment underneath the subway platform and darted inside. It was dead and dark, which is good for me. I propped myself up on the chair and nervously surveyed the area. Within minutes, I was staring into space as I generally do, with nothing but a glazed look and an empty mind. To my left was a seemingly normal, decently attractive man chatting civilly with the bartender. Somehow, as is always the case, I got roped into the conversation. And soon, the conversation between me, the bartender, and the man to my left became a conversation between me and the man to my left. As my new friend Michael and I chattered away about a great many topics of which we were mutually fond, I spent most of my time studying the features of his face than listening to the words coming out of his mouth.

"This guy is the lovechild of Chris Pratt and Eric Bana. He's probably my age. Maybe older. I'd say late 20's. 29. I was right. Of course. I know so many nearly 30 Michaels now. It's like I collect Michaels. Gosh, I love New York. You never know when you're just gonna hit it off with a stranger and talk about things that set your heart ablaze. I'm hungry."

"Ya wanna get tacos?" I bark, interrupting Michael mid-sentence with this question that was most assuredly irrelevant to anything he was saying.

"Uh, alright," he answered with some hesitation.

"Come on, I know a great taco truck around the corner," I explain as I pick up my twenty-five pound backpack and zip out of the Irish pub, not even looking behind me to make sure Michael is still there.

Following slightly behind, Michael entertained my chirping as I raved and ranted about the delicacies that came from the taco truck.

"Dos tacos de carnitas, por favor! Gracias, amigo!" I cry with an embarrassing Spanish accent.

"You speak Spanish?" Michael asks.

"What are you talking about?" I ask.

As we get our bag of tacos, I scurry over to the bench by the side of the road, unable to contain myself. I waste no time in shoveling half of a taco in my mouth and continuing to ramble away about tacos as my new friend looks on in bewilderment at the girl who, at 23, never learned it was rude to speak with her mouth full of food. After snarfing down two tacos and not taking even a second to stop talking, my eyes began to water. My nose started running. My face was turning beet red. I ignored all of these symptoms like a brave, yet inane little soldier and kept talking about every unimportant, whimsical notion that popped into my underdeveloped cranium. Eventually, my new friend cut me short.

"Are you OK?" he asks.

By now I am vehemently sniffling and real tears are streaming down my face, yet I still manage to ignore everything that is happening.

"I think I might need some water," I finally concede.

"Ok, there's a CVS across the street."

Before Michael could even finish his sentence, I had already gotten up off of the bench and was sprinting towards the pharmacy. Upon entering the store, I reached for the nearest beverage and ran to the self-checkout. I rummaged through my purse searching for money to no avail. There was Michael, standing beside me stoically, handing me crisp one dollar bill after one dollar bill like a human ATM machine. I frantically grabbed each one and uncoordinatedly and violently attempted to shove the dollar bills into the slot.

"You know you can drink that in here and then pay after," Michael reminded me.

Upon hearing this, I stopped everything I was doing and sucked every last drop of that lemonade out of the bottle.

While I, like a baby dinosaur discovering something for the first time, guzzled down my drink, Michael coolly and calmly inserted the dollar bills into the machine.

Still trying to recover from the heat, I plopped back down on the bench and stared into space, trying to catch my breath. I went right back to talking about frivolous things, putting on a brave face.

"Look, I don't mean to be rude or anything, but if you don't feel well, go home," Michael suggested. I looked at him. That was the first common sense idea I had been exposed to all night. I thanked him for the evening and went home.

I was sure I had scared Michael away for good, but it turns out we are neighbors and now friends. Poor Michael.

The Handsome Pilots

It was a brisk October afternoon.

My travel partner, Adriana, and I had just been dumped off at the Toronto Airport. Our flight was departing in a few hours and we would soon embark on our European backpacking trip (side note, on that trip I gained fifteen pounds courtesy of Italy).

While waiting for our flight, I threw a couple of sleeping pills down my wide open gullet so that I would be able to endure the excruciatingly dull hours on the plane. I so despise flying. Don't get me wrong. Taking off is great fun as is landing, but the part where you are just suspended in space for hours on end…that, I loathe. Who wants to be crammed into what is essentially a giant tuna can with a bunch of fat, smelly strangers that you instantly hate just because you're put in such close proximity to them? And what's worse, I'm constantly plagued by the thought of dying in a plane crash with these fat, smelly strangers. Even when I'm not on a plane, I think about this. It means that if I die on a plane, I die surrounded by a bunch of furry folks that I don't know, don't care to know, and know I don't like. That's no way to go. I need to die valiantly…a sniper's bullet to my head as I'm giving my commencement speech…some sort of hit job…something glamorous and noble. Anyway, I'm going off on a tangent.

As I was saying, I pop a couple pills because I hate flying. And I probably popped them a bit too early. One time I took a handful of sleeping pills at the crack of dawn just to see what life would be like drowsy on sleeping pills for a day. It was miserable and I partially learned my lesson from that. I remember spending the entire day staring at a wall and drooling before finally gathering enough energy to grab some Big Macs from McDonald's.

So there I was at the boarding gate in a vegetative state. My hood was up over my head, my dark sunglasses covered my eyes, and my face was filled with contempt as it generally is. As I sat there, limbs sprawled out all over the place, exiting the gate was a handful of handsome male pilots. Young ones too. All chipper and gay like they were Gene Wilder's backup tap dancers in some golden age Vincente Minelli film. The only thing that separated the men from me was a thick, glass wall. Upon seeing Adriana and me, the pilots smiled jovially, tipped their hats, and waved.

Stunned, Adriana leans over to me and inquires, "Are they waving at us?"

"Of course they are, darling," I mused, confidently, not moving a muscle. "Wave back now," I ordered as I flopped my rubbery hand up and down, waving at them as if I was Princess Diane.

They were indeed waving at us and frankly, I had no idea why. Now, Adriana is exotically beautiful so that probably had something to do with it. And when I'm not a drooling vegetable, I clean up pretty good.

I'm a proper 6 if I shower and put a little makeup on. So maybe they could see I had the potential to be a looker.

"Wow," my friend said under her breath. She seemed amazed. Of course I was too, because how often do handsome pilots flirt with you through the glass window of an airport? Never. I hid my amazement and acted like all of this was just a daily occurrence for me.

"Let me tell you something," I started, picking up my limp body and leaning in closer to Adriana as if I was telling her a secret (though I was loud enough for everyone at the gate to hear me). "Mennnnnnnn love me. Just stick with me, kid. There's plenty more where that came from."

And with this incongruent string of words, my friend looked at me disconcertedly. It was clear by the look on her face that she was horrified at what she had gotten herself into by being with me. And thus began our two month trek through Europe.

The One Story I'll Never Fully Understand Myself

Sometimes things happen to me that I just can't explain. On top of that, they are utterly pointless. This is the tale of a pointless thing that I can't explain happening to me and your life will be none the richer for knowing it. Stop now, if you don't want to lose any more brain cells.

At the start of this story, I would say the day began quite normally. As a freelance writer, I can turn any café into my office. So off I went to a local café/grocery store (AKA Wegmans AKA the place better than Whole Foods AKA cry into your wheat germs and overpriced Manuka honey you hairy, I'm-27-but-I-still-live-at-home-and-the-reason-I-still-live-at-home-at-27-is-because-I-spend-$14.99-on-manuka-honey hipsters. Just divorce Whole Foods already and come over to the Wegmans dark side, you Brooklynite trust fund brats who are sitting on the six figures your mom and dad made, but you dress like you're from The Civil War....I don't know where all of this snark is coming from.

So I'm at this café, minding my own business, diddling away on my laptop when suddenly I am approached by the kind of person that I'd expect would have severed body parts of women in the trunk of his car.

When he approached me he was nervous and sweaty, not because he was nervous to approach me (a solid 10…fine a 6 with makeup), but because there was something insidious festering beneath his squirrely surface.

"Excuse me, miss. C-could I ask you for a favor?"

And because I am a spineless pushover, I'll say "yes" to about anything.

"What?" I ask him.

"I was just at the customer service desk trying to return this item. I can't do it, so I wondered if you could do it for me."

This is the part where normal people say "no" or at the very least, request more information from the person making the odd plea. But no. I am an idiot who blindly obliges and questions nothing.

I shrugged, hopped out of my seat, took the bag from his hand, and began packing up my laptop.

"Oh I'll watch your laptop, while you go up to the front desk," offered the stranger.

I didn't question this at all. I just left my laptop and personal belongings with this person. Oh, but it gets even better. After I make this bizarre return for the guy (to this day I don't know what it was or why he couldn't return it himself), I come back and sure enough, he was still sitting there with my stuff.

"Here's your money," I say.

"Thanks so much. Do you think maybe I could get your number?"

I am the kind of stupid that you just can't make up. I always, always, always give out my phone number to strangers and I have no idea why. I just spit it out like at ATM machine dispensing cash. I have no control mechanism. A person could ask for my social security number and I would probably give it to them.

So I gave the weird little boy my number.

After he left, I found myself sitting there asking, "What just happened?"

A mere hour or so later, I received a text from the strange gentleman. I don't remember his name. All I can recall is that the area code was the same area code of an ex-boyfriend with whom I'd recently called it quits. I always thought that was weird, though it has nothing to do with the story.

I also don't recall any of the text message exchanges, but I'm fairly certain that at one point he asked if he could see me and I said something about how I'd just broken up with someone, so no.

That was the end of that. So I thought. This is where it gets a little weird (nonetheless, still pointless).

The evening of this bizarre incident, I met up with a couple of girlfriends over tea to tell them about the story.

Allow me to paint a picture of how sad and pathetic my hometown is. There is virtually nothing for an underage person to do in this impoverished, underpopulated region. So when you wanted to see your friends, you just had to work with what you got. My friend and I would routinely frequent a chain coffee shop in a seedy part of town where I later discovered lots of drug deals went on. We'd sit in the parking lot, drink our tea, and chat. We were wild animals.

As we sat in the car discussing the day's events, my phone went off. It was the stranger from earlier.

"Hey, I know this is kinda weird, but I could really use your help. My crazy ex-girlfriend found me and is following me and I need your help."

I read the message aloud to my friends.

"Isn't it odd that as soon as I tell you guys about this guy he texts me?" I blurt out. My friends agreed. I quickly typed a message back to the stranger.

"I'm sorry I can't help you, I'm busy at the moment."

"Where are you?" he replies, instantly.

I didn't respond.

He calls me. The three of us are beginning to get concerned. Every time I ignore his call, he calls again. He then texts me.

"Please just come. I need your help. I'm in Brooklyn Square."

And then the hair on the back of my neck stood up.

I was in Brooklyn Square.

"He followed me," I whispered to my friends as I ducked into the trunk of the vehicle. "How is he here?! Does he know I'm here? Drive the car, dive the car! Get outta here!"

To this day, I don't know who that man is, why any of that happened, or how he knew where I was.

The moral of the story is that sometimes things will happen in your life and you will have no idea why.

The other moral of the story is don't give your phone number out to random strangers or let them talk you into running odd errands for them.

*Edit: Looking back at all of this, I vaguely recall that the item I returned might have been some sort of medication. Maybe I was a useful idiot in some shady drug deal. Who knows? Probably not the first time I've unwittingly participated in a drug deal.

The Time I Thought My Friend Was Being Raped And Pillaged by a Stranger So Obviously I Called 911

It was a slow Saturday afternoon. I'm not sure what I was doing, but I am 100% certain that whatever it was it was a profound waste of time. Probably watching workout videos of hot babes doing squats in tiny shorts while I polished off my 39th pizza pocket. I do recall that a close girlfriend of mine was telling me that she was meeting a guy she was "kinda sorta" seeing, but she wasn't totally sure about the dude. I was instructed to answer any of her calls within the window of 1 PM to 4 PM because she was with him and if she was going to call me while she was with him it meant that something was wrong. In my mind, this meant the man was a psychopathic killer so I just filed that away in my mental rolodex.

It was after 3:30 PM when my friend texted me. All it said was "9-1-1". I jump into action. I could feel my heart pounding. I envisioned a million different circumstances in my head. She is hiding somewhere in her apartment texting me as the man hunts her down. They are in a struggle and she had just one second to text 911 to me and nothing else. I must call 911 for her.

I call. I am maniacal on the phone.

"Hello! Yes, hello?! My friend told me to call 911. There is a strange man in her house. She is alone with him. I don't know what is happening to her, but I know it's bad."

"OK, here does she live."

"..........."

"Ma'am?"

"Um, I, uh, I don't really know. I mean I know…I just don't know the address."

"Ok, what street is her house on?"

"……uh….I'm not really sure of that either. But can you please just send somebody over?! It's near the park. You know the park that I'm talking about? The one with the baseball field. And then there's a grocery store somewhere by there too. You gotta know what I'm talking about!!"

"Ok, I don't…can you give me any more details?"

"What more do you need to know?! It's a yellow house, there's a park across the street. The grocery stores is somewhere around there. Just go already!!"

"Ok, ma'am. How about this. How about you try getting a hold of your friend and asking her."

While this dialogue is occurring my friend had been calling me throughout it. I kept declining her phone call. I was so irritated. Here she is asking me to call 911 for her and I'm doing that and she knows I'm on the phone and suddenly she is calling me. What is that about?!

Finally I tell the officer I will call him right back and I answer my friend's incessant phone calls.

"Amy!! Are you OK? Is he still there? Why are you calling me when you know I'm on the phone? I can't talk to the police when you're calling me over and over again."

"What? Why are you talking to the police?"

"BECAUSE YOU TOLD ME TOO!"

"No I didn't..."

"YES YOU DID. You wrote 911 so I called 911!!!!!"

"Wait, you actually called 911?"

"WHY WOULDN'T I CALL 911???? You tell me that you are meeting a man you barely know in the privacy of your own home all alone, then you text me 911, and all I can imagine is you getting hacked to pieces with the rusty end of a curtain rod."

"I can't believe you actually called the police. I just meant for you to call me ASAP. I thought we used 911 to tell each other when we needed to speak to each other right away."

"We don't use 911!!!!! We say EMERGENCY! There is a difference! I just spent the last few minutes babbling on the phone with a switchboard operator about how my friend was getting raped by some guy near the park!"

My friend found all of this ridiculously funny and I was but slightly amused over time.

All you need to know about me is that if you are in trouble, you can count on me to take the initiative to do something about it, but you can fully expect that somewhere along the line I'm gonna mess things up.

Stacy, You Stupid Woman, You Owe Me $200

What pettiness I am about to write about will reveal to you what a sick little person I am. This has plagued me sporadically since I was 19. And to this day, mainly because I am a small-minded little person, I'm still irked by this. So much so, that I have decided to dedicate an entire section of my book to the person who screwed me over. The saddest part is that it isn't that big of a deal. But every once in a wee while it sneaks into my head and I'm filled with bitterness and rage over it. I know what you are thinking: I'm not mentally sound or healthy and I should devote my time to more productive matters but as I said, I'm a sick person. So four years ago, at the age of 19, I was working on a horse farm for an uppity brat of a woman who had everything in life handed to her on a silver platter including her pristine horse farm and the venture capital to start her little internet fabric business that naturally, mommy and daddy paid for. Maybe it comes down to the classic poor person hates the rich person who obtained their wealth through inheritance instead of work. The point is, it was clear that at the ripe ol' age of 35 or however old she was, stupid Stacy (I think that was her name) never had to do any heavy lifting in her life. Mommy and daddy gave her money and shiny things and that's how she got where she was in life. So anyway, I'm a 19 year old kid getting paid a couple bucks an hour to shovel horse crap all summer long. Now, I'm not doing 80 hour a week back breaking work, but scooping the fecal matter of twenty plus horses is relatively hard physical labor. At the time of 19 (and still sometimes today) I was always a timid pushover. I didn't know how to ask for things or speak my mind. I had absolutely no backbone. So when a week or two would slip by that stupid Stacy (stupid Stacy is her official name, by the way) would "forget to pay me my measly paycheck", I would just tell myself, "Oh she'll remember and I'll get it eventually". I know. Stupid. By the end of the summer, come quittin' time, I gave stupid Stacy my two weeks' notice. By this point, she still hadn't paid me for two weeks of work. I finally get a faux sense of courage to text her about it. She accuses me of just trying to milk more money out of her. Needless to say, I never got paid.

And there are two morals of the story: one is never work for stupid Stacy whatever-her-last-name-is at whatever-her-unmemorable-horse-farm is because she will rip you off. She also did a piss poor job of training the horses and relied on brute, Philistine tactics to force her horses into submission (can you tell I hate this woman?). The second is don't be like me at 19. Don't be a pushover. Don't expect that people will be nice or decent. Say what needs to be said and never feel bad about it. Don't apologizing for things you should never apologize for. Gosh, thinking about this makes me want to start seminars called the anti-stupid Stacy seminar on how to conquer your own spinelessness and get what you want out of life. Also, now that I've been thinking about it a little more, I'm not even sure the woman's name was Stacy, but Stacy is the name of ugly people and this woman was ugly so her name is Stacy in my mind.

The One Time in My Life I Felt Like I Was in an Episode of Friends

It was the Saturday morning after a historically bad first date with a pushy Turkish Muslim who, within fifteen minutes of us meeting, began acting like my keeper. After only an hour of knowing me, he told me, "I want you to be my girlfriend. I don't want you seeing anybody else".

"Wow. The first date isn't even over and I already have to break up with too!", I thought as I stared at him with a mix of disbelief and annoyance.

Fast forward to the following Saturday morning, I pulled myself out of bed, threw on a pair of jeans, and plopped along to the nearest café I could find. As I entered, I noticed I had been noticed. Now, when you come from a small town, everybody already knows you and has no interest in knowing you beyond what they already know. But when you have just moved to a big city, New York to be exact, people have no qualms about approaching complete strangers.

"Oh crap," I thought to myself as I could see from my peripherals that this man was staring in my general direction. It should be noted, I do not become irritated and standoffish at the prospect of men hitting on me because I'm oh-so-tired of them hitting on me and I'm just too good for them all, but because I am spectacularly anxious about the very idea that anyone would take interest in me. I would sooner shoot myself in my own face in a playground full of little children watching me and risk permanently emotionally scarring them for life than entertain the idea that someone might like me. This should give you some insight into how profoundly low my self-esteem is. I know me. I know how disgusting and bizarre I can be, why would I make anyone suffer through all of that? The man began approaching me and I could feel my chest tighten. My jaw clenched, my eyes widened, and my breath shortened. I felt like a ferret cornered in her cage.

"Hello," the man began.

I smiled nervously at him the way David Hyde Pierce smiles at Frasier when he has said something particularly saucy.

"I couldn't help but notice you and thought you were very beautiful".

"Oh thank you," I was able to spit out.

"I wondered if I might be able to take you to dinner some time?"

"Oh that is very nice of you, but---"

"But you have a boyfriend," he finished for me.

Yeah, sure, OK, we'll go with that.

"Well," I said with a shrug.

"Well, just in case anything changes, here is my phone number."

And he handed me a little piece of paper as I politely dismissed him.

What. Just. Happened? Did we just get transported to a 90's sitcom? In all my life I had never experienced a man brazenly stare, muster up the courage to approach me, ask me out to DINNER---not to, "um, ya know, like...hang out sometime maybe"---DINNER AND hand me his phone number on a piece of PAPER in the age of digital technology?

It all could have been quintessential if only the man had teeth (call me shallow, FINE) and if I had been a more grounded, self-assured individual.

Running Over Traffic Cones at 1 AM is as Fun as it Sounds (Possibly Illegal as Well)

When I was 18, I had this piece of crap car. And I know everyone will tell you that they had a piece of crap car when they were a teenager, but I bet it was never so bad that they had to routinely snatch their crowbar out of the backseat, hop out of their truck, and bang on this fancy little thing known as a solenoid starter until the car would start again. And you would bang and bang and bang the starter until finally, when you turned the key over, the vehicle would start running again. Many a traffic jam have I started with ol' Rusty blue (that is my 1999 Ford Ranger and I just came up with that; I have never used that name once). Every time my truck just *kerplunk!* stopped in the middle of the road (sometimes very busy roads) it was only a matter of seconds before the people in the vehicles behind me would see this 110 pound rodent-like creature adorned in a sun dress pounce onto the ground with crow bar in hand, scurry underneath the truck, and start whackin' away.

There are two vivid memories that come to mind regarding my solenoid starter (excluding the one where I taught my friend how to drive stick shift and she almost rolled my truck into a cop car behind us....that's a different story).

The one involves me prancing around half in the buff with little Amish children staring at me as if an alien had dropped from the sky.

The other involves what may have been illegal activity.

*Edit: I have since been informed it was illegal so as a disclaimer I would like to state that some stories in this book have been embellished or are entirely untrue, especially this one...*wink wink.

Anyway let's begin with the first story:

It was the summer I turned 17 (how alive I was, I think I peaked then which is as depressing as you'd imagine it would be). I was so gay and lively and spry. So full of life and always looking for the next adventure. On a hot July afternoon, I propped myself up in my pickup truck and drove to a godforsaken wasteland to pick up a girlfriend of mine for some summer shenanigans.

Of course I took a wrong turn and ended up in Amish country. And of course when I ended up in Amish country, far from cell phone service and modern day civilization, ol' Rusty blue pooped herself. What could I do but jump out of my truck and give the solenoid star a few good thwacks with my crowbar? I may have muttered a handful of unladylike words under my breath (or I may have shouted them loudly). After about ten minutes, I finally got the truck to start.

Unbeknownst to me, two little Amish boys had seen my entire performance. They just stared, jaws dropped, as they watched this strange lady scurrying about her truck, barefoot with a pair of shorts and a sports bra on, spouting off obscene swear words as she wiped the sweat from her brow.

After starting my car, peeling off the dirt road, and getting back on track, I passed a beautiful abandoned insane asylum that I, regrettably, have not yet been able to break into and trespass.

That was a bad day. Once I reached my friend, I practically pushed her into my truck and said, "Get in the car quick, we are never coming back to this place!"

The other time I can recall my car breaking down---of the many, many times that it did---was on a main road in my hometown where there was routinely heavy traffic. The traffic gets heavier when a small, blue pickup stops right in the middle of all the action and there is road work being done that hasn't been finished in three months. A car breaking down is always irritating; it is even more irritating when you have places to be and things to do. I was late for work when my car suddenly decided it would stop in traffic.

Banging away at my truck while old men in their semi-trucks and soccer moms in their minivans watched in amusement just made me even more frustrated.

After work, in the wee hours of the night, I got a hankering. I got a hankering to do something mildly destructive. I didn't know what, but I decided I wasn't going to bed until I could leave the world a wee bit more inconvenienced (I don't know why I keep writing "wee"; I'm either getting in touch with my Irish leprechaun or I've been holding in the pee too long).

After a long summer day, my friend and I piled into my truck and decided that going to the main road where construction had been held up for months and knocking down all of the traffic cones would be a good use of our time.

There we were. The wide open road. No cars. Just the dead of night and hundreds of orange traffic cones taunting us. Hundreds of cones that took up the street and held up traffic for months, put there by city workers who take what should be a six day project and turn it into a three month project. And we knocked down everything single one of them. My friend opened the passenger door and I opened my door as and we drove down the road we hit every single cone with our doors. I have never laughed so hard in my life. What can I say? Destruction gives me life. I acquiesce, there might be something evil living inside of me.

Was this juvenile? Certainly.

Do I regret it? No.

Would I do it again? Probably not.

So what can we learn from this? Though Shannon is an evil person and potentially a rudimentary psychopath, she has shown some signs of growth in emotionally and mental maturity. Some. Not a lot.

Turkish Delight

After a solo cultural field trip to the European market in my neighborhood and close to thirty minutes of aimlessly strolling the aisles pretending I knew what I was doing, I happened upon a box of sweets that looked enticing enough to purchase. In fact, upon seeing these mystery delights, I noticed myself salivating as I stared at the picture on the front of the box. Suddenly, I began to feel like Edmund in Narnia. After all of these years, I finally understood why this little English twerp was so enraptured by Turkish delight. It was as though I was looking at a silver platter filled with little pieces of Turkish delight. As I stood there in a daze, studying the fineries of this candy box, I took it all in: the white confectionary sugar-coated nuggets, the piping hot cup of tea in a silver cup, the meticulously engraved platter, all on a regal white backdrop with bold red lettering and a stately design of various patterns.

"I'm gettin' 'em," I said to myself as I brusquely grabbed the box off of the shelf. "$4.99 Ok. That's fine. I can't afford to buy eggs for 99 cents, but whatever, I can gamble away five bucks on candy I've never had or heard of before."

After purchasing my items at the checkout, I sauntered back to the sweltering sidewalk and made my way to the train. Like a rodent seen digging through the dumpster in the back alley of a Chinatown restaurant, I clawed at the saran wrapped box until I was able to successfully remove all of the plastic. I popped off the lid and experienced my first taste of Lokum which really was Turkish delight after all. Remnants from the explosion of confectionary sugar landed all over my face, chest, and shirt. I nearly spit it all out. "I'm eating the poop of vengeful fairies." I hadn't ever tasted anything so repulsively sweet in my life.

I could not believe that this was something sold to people or that people would actually eat it. The texture frightened me. So I had another. And it was just as disgusting as the first time. Maybe a little more so now.

I vowed I would never touch another piece of Turkish delight again. I tucked it away in my kitchen cabinet and planned to gift my friend with it, someone I knew would actually appreciate this Middle Eastern treat.

But one evening, out of boredom, I cracked open that stupid box of Lokum. Everything about food, no matter how disgusting that food is, becomes so much more appealing after 11 PM.

"Just one," I tell myself.

I eat one. Then I ate sixteen. Then I ate the whole box.

"You know this isn't as bad as I remember it being," I said as I shoveled my sixth, seventh, eighth piece in.

It was done. I finished off the entire box. I look down at myself, my stomach several centimeters wider that it was ten minutes earlier, with a sheet a cocaine white powder all over me.

"Now you've done it. Just look at yourself. How can you be proud? No, but I am. I ate all of these without going into hypoglycemic shock or vomiting all over the place. That's an accomplishment. Ok, actually no matter what way you look at this, you are the human equivalent of an obese squirrel who discovered crack cocaine. You look like Templeton from 'Charlotte's Web'."

The moral of the story is, it doesn't matter how disgusting I find a type of food. If it's sitting in front of my face, I'm gonna eat. And I'm gonna eat all of it.

About The Author:

I'm just your garden variety idiot.

Made in the USA
Middletown, DE
30 July 2017